Pink Ribbons for April

*For Paul and Coral
and the people of Machynlleth*

Pink Ribbons
for April

In Memory of
April Jones

Alun Gibbard

yl **Lolfa**

First impression: 2013

© Copyright Alun Gibbard and Y Lolfa Cyf., 2013

The publishers wish to acknowledge the support of
Cyngor Llyfrau Cymru

Cover design: Y Lolfa

ISBN: 978 184771 709 2

'Mum' written by Polly Peters, from *Mad, Bad and Dangerously Haddock*
by Andrew Fusek Peters (Lion Hudson, 2006)
© Andrew Fusek Peters & Polly Peters
by permission of Lion Hudson PLC

'Progress' by Alan Gillis, from *Somebody, Somewhere* (2004)
by permission of the author and The Gallery Press,
Loughcrew, Oldcastle, County Meath, Ireland

'Seren' by permission of Tudur Dylan Jones
'Daughter' by permission of Gillian Clarke
'Waiting' by permission of Ruth Burgess

With thanks to Iestyn Hughes and *The Daily Post*
for generously providing so many photographs
and also to April's family for photographs of April

FSC
Published and printed in Wales
on paper from well maintained forests by
Y Lolfa Cyf., Talybont, Ceredigion SY24 5HE
website www.ylolfa.com
e-mail ylolfa@ylolfa.com
tel 01970 832 304
fax 832 782

Weep with me, all you that read
This little story:
And know, for whom a tear you shed
Death's self is sorry.
'Twas a child, that so did thrive
In grace and feature,
As heaven and nature seem'd to strive
Which own'd the creature.

Ben Jonson

'She fought to come in to this world, she fought to stay in this world, and he has taken her, not only from us, but from everyone who loved her. I will never see her smile again or hear her stomping around upstairs on to the landing. We will never see her bring her first boyfriend home and Paul will never walk her down the aisle. How will we ever get over it?'

Coral Jones, April's mum

Acknowledgements

THIS IS A sensitive story – one which needs the support and cooperation of many in its writing. These are my personal, practical thanks. The writing was often difficult and personal support was highly valued. Writing in isolation on such a subject proved, at times, to be painful and even impossible. It was essential, therefore, to flee from solitary writing at home and write among the distraction of other people's busyness. That meant, for me, working in an Italian eating place in Llanelli, Altalia, in order to have the comfort of other people around me. Thanks to Tal, Alex, Brigitte, Dion and Sion for understanding the lone writer in the corner and for the support I had.

The people of Machynlleth have been immense and a similar kind of support was also received from those who work at the Wynnstay Hotel in the town. They gave me the space I needed.

I wish to thank the Welsh Books Council for backing this book and Y Lolfa publishers for their invaluable editorial support throughout the whole process.

I have had great support and interest from good friends and I value that immensely; suffice it to name Andrew, Stuart, Emma and Jo. But the biggest support, both emotional and practical, came from Fiona. She has read the text and commented constructively on it; she has put up with the demands on my time to go to Machynlleth, and with the draining of my emotions in dealing with such a subject. She's been there to hold my hand.

Diolch o galon, cariad.

Alun Gibbard
September 2013

Contents

Preface: Lanterns in the sky   11

1   First day of October, last days of April   16

2   'Please! Please! My daughter's been kidnapped!'   27

3   A tragic twist, a change of plan   45

4   This small, quiet town   57

5   Healing words and hugs   78

6   A place to talk   90

7   We can't all search for little April   103

8   The pity and the poetry   120

9   How will we ever get over it?   134

10   April's Law   152

11   A fragile hope   158

Lanterns in the sky

'IT'S TOO SOON!' – the heartfelt cry made by some on hearing that this book was a work in progress. They wished no ill-will, but were certain that the time was not right for the story of what happened to April to be told in full. And in one real sense, of course, it is too soon. Feelings are still raw, there is still confusion as to why what happened took place, and how could it occur in a place such as Machynlleth. The feeling changed from 'something like that will never happen here' to 'if it can happen here, it can happen anywhere'. The trial was only concluded a few months ago, the media circus has only just rolled out of town, the outside interest has only just started to wane with the townspeople only just beginning to find the rhythm to their day-to-day life that was normality at the end of September last year.

But without being disrespectful to those who feel that it's too soon, there is a need to put pen to paper. There is a precedent for doing so. Within a year of the disaster at Aberfan in 1966, for example, a book was published to tell the story of the horrors that that village suffered in losing 116 of its children. But this book was not written to dwell on the horrors committed by Mark Bridger or the shattering effect those deeds had on the people of Machynlleth. Rather, it has been written to note how a community, violently thrown into such a situation, dealt with it, coped, and began to move on. It's a testimony to community spirit rather than a dwelling on the evil acts of one man.

This book is a first response; an initial attempt to chronicle a community's reaction to tragedy. Just as hundreds of lanterns were released into the sky as symbols of hope for April – an attempt to send small flickering lights into an unending darkness – so this book aims to show the light that the people of Machynlleth shone into the evil of this story by the way they responded.

Sitting at home watching the unfolding story, I was struck by the way that April's neighbours reacted to her plight. There was something special happening in the midst of extreme sorrow. It was rare to see such pulling together and, as one with no links at all with the Dyfi Valley, I felt a pride in their actions; I was warmed by their spirit. That's where this book came from.

The next task was knowing how to approach a community under affliction. A prominent local figure in the rolling news story was Kathleen Rogers, the town's vicar. I thought therefore that the best way in was through the Church in Wales. I contacted a friend within that establishment, Randolph Thomas, who was at that time the archdeacon of the diocese of Brecon. He told me to contact his counterpart at the Bangor diocese which I did and obtained Kathleen Rogers' number. Therefore, with full hierarchical Episcopal backing, I tentatively made that first phone call to her and explained my intentions. I had a warm reception and we arranged to meet. From then on, after many discussions and much questioning, I have received nothing but complete support. She is not a public person, for all the trappings of the high profile role that she's had to play in front of the watching world since 1 October last year. I know that she, like so many others at the heart of this story, will struggle with reading this full account and might not do so for quite some time. But the support for it has been unwavering.

As it has been from the then town mayor, Gareth Jones. His support and contribution has been unquestionable. I have been given an insight into the heartbeat of Machynlleth through conversations with him that have informed my interpretation of his town and his people on these pages.

With both Kathleen and Gareth, their support and input has been as noted, but they are in no way responsible for the editorial content of this book. That's down to me.

Once the work was underway, many visits were made to Machynlleth. The story of the town's response began to unfold. It became apparent early on that there were many stories, many anecdotes, many opinions. A way of working, a modus operandi, was needed. I decided that I would not include a story that was heard only from one person. It would have to be said more than once over a period of time for it to be included.

Many of the townsfolk have been extremely cooperative and very welcoming. I am so grateful for that. I have responded to the wishes of many of them and respected their anonymity.

Thanks also to Mike Parker, Professor Jenny Kitzinger and Carolyn Hitt for their conversations about the issues April's story raises.

As time went on, the people of Machynlleth went through various stages in their grieving. They still do, of course, and it's quite likely they will be at another stage when this book comes out. During the writing, this often meant that I was asking questions about the way they felt at a particular period of the story's unfolding, but they were themselves feeling differently by then. This often led to them being unable to share recollections with me, not a reluctance, but an understandable emotional inability to think back once they had moved on. The various stages in their grief are dealt with on these pages.

A major concern in the early days of research was not wanting April's parents, Coral and Paul, to find out about the existence of a proposed book accidentally, through word of mouth, on the streets. I forwarded a message to Kathleen Rogers to pass on to the police family liaison officer, who in turn would inform Coral and Paul. I received an answer from them saying that they were happy for me to write the book. Some months later, while in Machynlleth, I was told that they were willing to meet me.

I shall never forget the afternoon I walked towards their home, accompanied by Kathleen Rogers. It was the first time that I had visited Bryn y Gog, the estate that I had seen so often in newspapers and on television. I am not unfamiliar with visiting scenes where bad things have happened, through work with BBC News. But this was different. We had been told to go round to the back of the house. This meant going past garages similar to those elsewhere on the estate from where April was taken. It was so stark, so real a feeling. And there, around a table in the back garden, sat Paul and Coral. Getting to them meant opening the gate that April had ran excitedly through on that fateful day in October last year, never to be seen again by Coral and Paul.

We sat and talked, but knowing how to be 'natural' in their company was not easy, however experienced a journalist I was. They were so welcoming. So dignified. It was very humbling. I leant over the table we sat around, with coffee in hand, and Paul turned to me, referring to a plant pot that my right hand was touching.

'That's the last Mother's Day present April gave Coral,' he said. I froze. A cold chill went through me. The whole situation became vibrant with significance and meaning and, above all else, abject sadness.

Other meetings with them have followed and they have been extremely supportive. It became evident though that no lengthy conversations with them could be included in the book. It was, in their case – the case that really counted – too soon. Their story will be told in time. Suffice for me to say that I am truly and sincerely grateful for the way that Coral and Paul have reacted to me and the idea of this book. I have nothing but the greatest admiration for them both. I have no idea how this book will play into their story, their thoughts, feelings and emotions. Coral turned to me at one time, and looked at me asking, very unassumingly and tentatively, whether I would be able to give them a copy of the book when it was finished. I told her that I would do so. But whether they read it or not, this book is for her and her husband because it's a story that they feel and understand in a way that no other person on earth can get near to understanding.

1

First day of October, last days of April

MONDAY, 1 OCTOBER 2012. New month, new week, new day. Early morning, in one of the houses on an estate on the eastern side of a mid Wales town, a five-year-old little girl wakes up tired and complaining of a bad tummy. Her mum goes into her bedroom to see her and gives her a big *cwtsh*, the Welsh word for hug or cuddle, and tells her everything's going to be all right, in a loving motherly way.

April had been born prematurely, at 34 weeks, weighing four pounds two ounces, and she had a hole in her heart. She was in intensive care for two weeks. By the time she was three years old, her parents were beginning to see that their little one was bumping into things, in a clumsier way than they would expect. They took her to the doctor and, after the necessary series of tests, the family were told that she had mild cerebral palsy, from her hip to her leg. Because her condition was diagnosed when she was so young, for a short period of time she took part in a trial for treatment to try to cure the condition. It meant that she had to wear a special kind of suit to protect her growing bones. Her mum and dad would massage her afflicted leg regularly and make sure that she did the exercises she was required to do every day. She needed daily medication for her condition. Because of this routine of care, her mother would say that the little girl ruled their lives – in the nicest way possible. She was not a sickly child, however. She would be described as slight for her age, yes. But by that October day, she had clearly shown that she was determined not to let her medical condition hold her back and she was full of life and doing everything her friends did.

That morning, the mum's magic touch works, the little girl feels better, and was out of bed and getting ready as normal to go to school. Her mum dressed her and tied her hair in a plait while her dad made the breakfast and her brother and sister got on with his day. Dressed in her school uniform and suitably fed, she was out of the house as normal, her dad taking her to school. She was less than a month into her new school year and it was a new world for her and her friends. When she got to Ysgol Gynradd Machynlleth (Machynlleth Primary School) she was ready to start a new week with her fellow five-year-olds in a school that was a world of colour, sound, stories and play to each and every one of them.

In a whitewashed cottage, Mount Pleasant, next to the trickling river Dulas in nearby Ceinws, one of the many hamlets haphazardly surrounding the main hub of the town, a man in his mid-40s wakes from disturbed sleep and, when it's nearly twenty-to-eight in the morning, he sees a text on his mobile phone.

'Couldn't leave it without saying goodbye. You were my love. Just can't do it. Maybe see you around, OK.'

'You were my life, babe. My everything. For what it's worth I'm still in love with you.'

'I do love you, just can't do it, sorry. I don't want anything from the house, OK.'

'So there's nothing left at all worth fighting for?'

'I said what I needed to say. Goodbye. This time, find the right woman for you. See you around. I'll miss you. Take care, babe. Love, Vicky.'

'Goodbye. Look after yourself and be careful. You don't have to change your number. I won't be hassling you.'

His girlfriend of only a few months has just dumped him. Things had been fairly rocky between them when they saw each other the day before, and they'd had words. He'd moved to live in that cottage a few weeks earlier, in the hope that his girlfriend would move in there with him and his border collie. She had moved in for a few days but left again and now it was all over. It was the start of a new week for him, as a single man.

From such normal beginnings, man and child carry on with their day.

The child spent her day at the school; children's babble and bustle filling the hours. Her mother spent the day shopping and then turned up at the school to collect her daughter, along with her husband. After a full day at school, at the beginning of a new week, the little girl was tired and a little grumpy. But she soon cheered up when her parents told her that she was going for her swimming lesson and her best friend was going too. She was greatly excited as she knew that meant going to the town's Leisure Centre, on the approach to the town from the south. In such a small town, the Leisure Centre played an important part in the social life of its citizens. Before the day was out, it was to play a role it had never imagined possible in all the days since it opened.

In the centre's welcoming pool, the little girl was in the early stages of mastering the strokes that would keep her safe in the water and give her so much fun. Then, lesson over, she was out and before there was time to dry properly, she was up and away and back home to have her tea. It was spaghetti on toast that night. Once fed, she was off again, to her best friend's house, where the two girls played happily upstairs and where they watched the film *Tangled* – a film in the true Disney tradition, about a princess whose mother is not willing for her to go where she wants to go and which ends up with an unsavoury thief taking her to a world she has never seen. It was her favourite film.

Then, back home, with the October night already drawing in, the five-year-old, still full of energy, wanted to go out to play with some of her friends on the Bryn y Gog estate. She nagged her parents, in the way only little five-year-olds can, asking them for permission to go out on her bike, as she had done countless times before. Originally, dad said that she couldn't, and that's when pester-power kicked in and she begged and nagged both mum and dad to let her go out. In the end, they gave in, motivated by the fact that the little girl had received a really good report in school, reluctantly giving in to her request as a way of showing that they were pleased with her. They also had the reassurance of knowing that the estate, designed as it was, was a safe place, where all the houses looked out on the area where the children usually played. The little girl was wearing her white school polo shirt, black trousers and her mother put a purple padded coat on her little girl, with fur round the outside of the hood, and zipped it up. Joyfully, with a big smile, she ran out of the house, picking up her pink bike on the way, opening the wooden gate at the bottom of the path and went out to play with her friends.

The man too had watched a film that day after things had gone horribly wrong for him. He phoned his boss to say that he wouldn't be in to do his work at a local hotel because he needed to have the time off in order to 'get his head around things'. He'd done lots of different jobs over the years, from swimming pool attendant at the Leisure Centre where the little girl had her lesson that day, to working in a slaughterhouse, in the bar and kitchen of a hotel, in forestry, as a welder, a car mechanic and a bouncer. He had been known, by the rest of the lads he knew in the town's pubs, to brag that he'd been in the SAS as well.

He wasn't a Machynlleth man. He was born in Carshalton in Surrey, into a respectable middle-class family. His father was a policeman, and a Royal Protection Officer. He had a brother and a sister who did better than him at school. But he drifted through education with remarkable anonymity. Soon, he would start trying to make his mark in his own way and fell victim of that overused cliché, 'falling in with the wrong crowd'. He faced his first trial in court in 1984, at the Old Bailey, charged with theft and firearm offences. He was on probation for two years after that.

By the time he was 20, he had fathered his first child, but fled from his partner before their child was born, leaving her to bring up the baby on her own. He moved to Wales, where he had been several times as a child on family holidays, specifically to Blaenau Ffestiniog in Snowdonia. When he got there, he told people that his parents had died, his father from a heart attack and his mother through suicide because she couldn't live with the grief of losing her husband. They are both still alive.

For a while, he lived in a tent on the beach near Porthmadog. He got a young woman from that area, a 17-year-old, pregnant, but that relationship didn't last. Following that another young woman and her child were left again.

In 1990 he moved for the first time to Machynlleth, fleeing the angry family of the 17-year-old he impregnated. That was the beginning of his long association with the town. He'd met another young woman while working at a hotel in Machynlleth and he married her, eventually moving to live with her in Machynlleth, her home town, after a spell of living in Wrexham. True to form, that relationship eventually ended too, this time after eight years. But he stayed on in Machynlleth, despite not wanting to have anything to do with the two sons he had from that marriage, even though they lived in the same small town among a population of 2,000 people.

Some time later, he thought that emigrating would sort his life out for him and he left Wales to start afresh in Australia. But the new life, the new him, wasn't to be found on the other side of the world either, and he returned after three months there. He came back to Machynlleth, went from job to job, had two further relationships, but no children this time.

So that's how he was in Machynlleth on that first day of October; a familiar part of the town's day-to-day scene, a man described by the local people as not looking out of place on the town's streets. They saw him as a man who had moved into the area, did this and that for a living and drank in the town's pubs. He was known to be light-fingered and often had goods to sell for cash. He was known for his tall stories, but they were never dark or sinister, just fabrications, fantasies on a mediocre and mundane scale. There were other stories of him, real ones, doing some unusual things occasionally, like going away to camp for weekends with only a crate of beer as luggage. He once changed his name to Mark 'Buster' Verona, adopting the surname of the first woman he got pregnant before fleeing from his paternal responsibilities to Wales. That was a strange enough move for a man who had completely abandoned her. His explanation for the name change was even more bizarre, but no less believed by those he told. Why wouldn't it be? He told his acquaintances that the Army had given him the name change in order to protect him from the IRA, because he had run over a member of that group in Northern Ireland. He would once more fall back on the 'running someone over' story in the years to come.

But that day, there was nothing to do but deal with what had been dealt to him. While the morning was still young, as a means of trying to get over being dumped, he contacted three different women he knew, asking them if they would come out for a drink with him. He obviously didn't intend to let any grass grow under his feet and moving on to someone else – anyone else – was the way to deal with the end of a relationship, even before it had grown cold. After all, he was used to it, never having held down a relationship for a very long time, and having six children from four different women. He was confident enough of his ability to attract the opposite sex and always had women on stand-by to turn to if, or rather, when, relationships didn't work out. He'd received no positive replies from the three he'd turned to that day to help him get over his 'loss'.

He sent these messages to the three women:

'Hadn't realised you were single, as I am. Do you fancy a drink or a club or even a meal? See how you feel.'

'Do you fancy a drink and a chat some time? No strings, OK.'

'Hi. Would you like to go out for a meal or a drink?'

He drank cider. He turned to the Internet. He turned to women he didn't know. He sent messages on social networking sites asking for no-strings-attached fun.

He also had images on his laptop that he turned to. He trawled through some files he had put together, which included photographs of young girls, children, some of whom were from Machynlleth and were friends of some of his children. He had images of children being abused and raped in some of these files too.

After a while, he left his cottage and headed to Machynlleth. Late that morning, he went to the headquarters of Powys County Council in Canolfan Hyddgen, next to Bro Ddyfi Comprehensive School, and in the shadow of Y Plas mansion (next door to the Leisure Centre) – another building that would take on a far greater significance as the day wore on. He had an issue to raise with the local authority. He wasn't happy with a summons he'd received for non-payment of his council tax and wanted everyone to know that. But he didn't get very far and he left disgruntled, before going back home again.

Later, at 12.59 p.m., he texts the girlfriend who had dumped him earlier that day. Obviously a change in mood had happened.

'Where are you? Well, didn't take you very long to tell everyone and move on.'

'No point lying to ppl. Why? Who you seen then?'

'I couldn't have meant **** all to you. Never mind.'

He was evidently oblivious to the hypocrisy of his actions in contacting other women already. It seems he hadn't taken long to get over the relationship either, but that wasn't the point for him.

Back home, he watched a film that was as far removed from the Disney film the little girl watched as it was possible to be. He watched what's referred to as a 'slasher' movie. Any definition of a slasher movie will include the words horror, psychopath, graphic and violence. It will include the words axe and knife as well. The violence that occurs is often dished out during or after sexual activity. The sole surviving hero at the end of such a film is very rarely any of the women who have been in the them.

That day, the man watched an animated slasher film, which was full of gratuitous sex and violence. One such film, regarded as a cult work within its genre, *The Last House on the Left*, had been recorded on his VCR when it was shown on Film4 some months earlier. He then recorded it again when it was on Film4+1. It was paused on one specific scene. It was a horrific scene of a young girl, tied and bound, being sexually abused. That was his viewing that day.

Then, fuelled by the images he'd seen, the rejection he thought he'd experienced, the sheer nothingness of his day and the twisted view he had of the world and himself, he left his cottage and set out for Machynlleth in his Land Rover Discovery once again, the laptop with the horrific images on it, in his vehicle with him.

At the end of the afternoon he visited Machynlleth Primary School in order to check on the progress of his eight-year-old daughter at the school. He had a ten-year-old son at that school as well. He stayed for about 20 minutes and it was obvious that he had been drinking. The little girl's parents were there too, while she was at her swimming lesson, and they were told that she was doing 'really well' in her class.

For a brief while that afternoon, the man and the child's parents were in the same building, hearing reports about their children's progress in school, before carrying on with the rest of their day; the family back to their home, the man on his lonely way.

Some time later, he found himself on the Bryn y Gog estate, where he was well known. He had lived there at one time with a 15-year-old girl with whom he went on to have two children, a son and a daughter. Two of his sons still live there. Another girlfriend and her mother lived there too, a few doors from April's house. During the course of the previous few months, he had become a lot friendlier with Paul, the father of April, as well. He'd helped him fix his car, and he'd also helped him to fix his children's bikes.

Bridger drove round and round for quite a long time that evening of the first of October, talking to some of the children he came across. He asked one young girl, who was ten years old, if she wanted to come to his house for a sleepover that night, a request made in the name of one of his children.

It was here that he made his fateful meeting with the five-year-old girl who had, until then, enjoyed her lovely day. Mark Bridger then took April Jones.

She climbed into his Land Rover Discovery, happy and smiling, according to the seven-year-old friend who was with her at the time. Her parents had taught her about 'stranger danger' and were confident that she wouldn't go into a car with anyone she didn't know. But more than that, April knew the man as a friend of her dad's who would fix their bikes and who always had sweets or a packet of crisps for her. She had no reason not to like him. A neighbour of April's family saw them drive off the estate at some speed. That was 20 minutes after her mum had zipped up her coat and she ran out to play. She would not be seen again, alive or dead.

That's how one child's normal day, indeed her life, can end, if one man sets his evil mind to it. Until that day, in addition to his appearance at the Old Bailey as a 20-year-old, he had been charged once with battery and using threatening words against the mother of two of his children; charged for assaulting a neighbour suffering from cancer in 2007; and convicted of assaulting a man in a pub. Such actions suggested that he was an unsavoury character and there were strong hints that he was not as he portrayed himself to the women he tried to charm or the men he shared a pint with. But they were offences that would be regarded as petty in the grander scale of criminal justice. This time though, he had committed a horrendous atrocity, completely off the scale of human behaviour.

It's the family, obviously, who felt the full impact of such a tragedy more than anyone else. Their strength, courage and quiet dignity in the face of such a horrendous event has been evident throughout the massive public exposure they've endured following the taking of their daughter – by a man they knew. As well as getting to know Paul Jones better in the months before April was taken, Bridger had met both Coral and Paul as soon as he moved to Machynlleth. Mark Bridger met Coral before she married Paul, while she was married to one of the men working in the town's Indian restaurant. Bridger and Coral played darts in the same pub. In 1996, the 29-year-old Bridger had a close link with Paul Jones, the man who was to become April's father. The 15-year-old girl he started dating and later lived with and had two children with, was the sister of Paul Jones's girlfriend at the time. Paul had two daughters with her, half-sisters of April's. Bridger had two children by the younger sister, a son and a daughter. Mark Bridger and Paul Jones knew each other. They were nearly family. That's whose daughter he took; that's whose daughter he killed.

Bridger and his victim started their day apart, in their own homes. Known to each other, and it shouldn't have been more than that. They met. He took her. He kept her. He killed her. What else he did we can only imagine. Fate didn't bring them together, evil intention did. An evil intention that ripped a young child from her loving family and ripped the life out of that same child. It was an act of evil that took the life of a child who was precious to her family, irreplaceable – and a child the town regarded as one of its own, as it regards all its children.

2

'Please! Please! My daughter's been kidnapped!'

AT SEVEN O'CLOCK that evening, April is playing with her friends near the garages not far from her home on the estate. They leave there and walk another friend back to her home and, when they return, Mark Bridger's car is parked nearby and he's standing a short distance away from his vehicle. April has a chat with him. After all, he was a man she knew well enough as he had been in her house many times in the months before that day. April's friend then sees her get into the vehicle with him. Another neighbour sees the Land Rover Discovery drive off the estate at what he thought was some considerable speed.

Back in the family home, mum Coral sends April's ten-year-old brother Harley out to look for her, to tell her that it's time to come home. It is twenty-past-seven. He's soon running back into the house in an awful state, hysterically trying to tell his parents what he's learnt while he was out. Coral calmly, but equally frantically, tries to calm her son down to get the story out of him. Eventually he is able to say enough for his mother and father to understand that April's friend has said that his sister has gone into a car with another man. Coral races to talk to the child herself and she confirms the story. Nine minutes after sending her son out to look for April, Coral makes a 999 call. This is the transcript of the call a frantic mother makes that night. The distress she is under is obvious, even if it's only from the way the operator has difficulty understanding what Coral is saying:

Coral Jones: 'Please, please! Please! My daughter's been kidnapped... my daughter, my daughter...'

Operator: 'Hang on a second, tell me again, what did you say, your dog has been kidnapped?'

Coral Jones: 'My daughter was out playing with a friend and she's been kidnapped.'

Operator: 'You've been kidnapped?'

Coral Jones: 'No, my daughter, she's five years old.'

Operator: 'Right, bear with me; it's not a very good signal.'

Coral Jones: 'No, I've got to go. Hang on; can you speak to them please?'

Coral hands the phone to a friend of hers, Valerie Jones.

Operator: 'Right, and what makes you think the daughter's been kidnapped?'

Valerie Jones: 'She's gone off in a car with somebody; somebody's picked her up in a car or something.'

Operator: 'What's the name of your daughter, can I take the name?'

Valerie Jones: 'She's not my daughter, she's my friend's daughter. She's gone, panicking, looking.'

Operator: 'OK, what's the name of the child who's gone missing?'

Valerie Jones: 'April Jones.'

Operator: 'April Jones, how old is she?'

Valerie Jones: 'Five.'

Operator: 'OK and this happened just literally minutes ago, did it?'

Valerie Jones: 'Minutes ago, yes.'

Operator: 'And the person that was able to tell you she got into the car, have they got details of the vehicle?'

Valerie Jones: 'She said it's a big grey car with a man driving. Everybody's just scattered everywhere to go and look now and I'm just by the house.'

Operator: 'Is there anything else you can tell us at the moment?'

Valerie Jones: 'No. Wait, wait, they're coming, they're coming...'

In the background, the operator can hear different people shouting across each other, against a backdrop of chaos.

'Come home, somebody's kidnapped April, just come home please...'

'Somebody's kidnapped April, somebody's kidnapped April...'

'She's gone...'

Almost everyone on the estate was out looking for the missing little girl. It was that sort of community. One single mother, a close neighbour of April's family, who wishes not to be named, had a knock on her back door early on that evening. Two people were there asking if she had seen April because the little girl hadn't gone home as she was supposed to. The mother told them that April had called there just over an hour earlier, to ask her son to go out to play. That wasn't possible and April had left. The mother hadn't seen April since then. Not long after that, the mother looked out of her window and saw a very large crowd gathering on the grass in front of her house. She realised that something important was happening and rushed out to see what that was, and what could be done.

'It was a really strange sight to be honest, and I'd not seen anything like it at all before on our estate. By then, hundreds of people were standing around, concerned for April; there was a quiet sort of noise that was moving around, the noise of the gathering crowd. But we weren't sure what to do. We discussed what we all thought could have happened, to try and make sense of things and maybe that would help us know what to do next. We thought that she might have got stuck behind one of the garages at the backs of the rows of houses on Bryn y Gog, or that she had wandered too far away from where she usually would play.'

Another mother on the estate thought that April had wandered the hundred yards or so from the lane at the back of the row of houses which included her home, and onto the main road that leaves Machynlleth towards Newtown. Others suggested that she was probably at a friend's house oblivious to all that was going on.

'But all these thoughts were slowly disappearing into the background as time was going on, especially the ones that were to do with her being somewhere on the site. Nearly everyone who lived there was out on the grass in the centre. There was no sign of her there, but we didn't start to think anything bad at that point.'

Meanwhile, in the town, a son was phoning his mother, to share the same news.

'I'd just got back from having been out for the evening and went on the computer, as you do, and this image kept cropping up of a little girl that had gone missing. Her face kept on cropping up really regularly and after a few minutes it dawned on me that this actually was a local child. I looked into it further then, of course, and then went over to tell my mother.'

That's how Kathleen Rogers, vicar of St Peter's Church, Machynlleth, came to hear of April's disappearance. She was at home that evening, busy preparing the Thanksgiving service for the following Sunday when her son called. She was in the process of thinking of new ways to conduct such a traditional service.

'My son had seen the story on Facebook and when I went to his house to see that page, not having it myself, I recognised the little girl straight away and said, "Oh, that's Coral's little girl!" I sort of knew Coral through the school, although I didn't know her very well. So we went up to Bryn y Gog and I couldn't believe the sight before us when we got there. Firstly, it was the sheer number of people congregating on the grass outside Paul and Coral's house and on the roads to the rest of the estate. Then came a growing realisation that we were all there for the same reason, people who mostly didn't know each other. We knew that in one way already of course, but we began to realise its implication as time went on. Seeing so many people there, because a little girl had been missing for a relatively short time, was quite something.

'We stood around aimlessly for what seemed like a long time because, while we all knew why we were there, we weren't too sure what we were supposed to do. We sort of looked at each other, chatted politely to each other, in a kind of "so now what do we do?" way.'

John Rogers went to speak to the one police officer who had been sent in those early hours to the Bryn y Gog estate. He told her that he was the relief local operations manager in the area for Network Rail, and asked if there was any way he was able to help with specific reference to the work he did.

'What I did then, off my own back, as the policewoman was in no position really to authorise anything, was to contact our control in Cardiff, ask them to page a description of April on Tannoys in train stations. I also asked them to do the same with Arriva Trains Wales. I then put another page out to all the staff, asking them to be vigilant on their way to and from work.'

Gradually, and in a way that's difficult to describe, people started to organise themselves into spontaneous groups and decide among themselves who was going to look where.

Those who were among the first to congregate at Bryn y Gog were there because they thought that a little girl had gone missing. They didn't know that inside their home, Paul and Coral had already made that 999 call, and that the fact that April had been *taken* had been established. In time, that news slowly trickled out to the concerned crowd outside and the whole mood changed.

'I panicked completely then,' a single mother-of-two said, 'and phoned my eldest son and told him to lock himself in the house. The youngest was with me. He's friendly with April's brother. Then it seemed as if things moved on really quickly. The police got involved and called us all to congregate at Huw Lewis' garage, near the Top Chippy, not far from the estate on the side of the road to Newtown. From there we made our way down to the town itself, about a mile away.

'But to be honest, even after being told that April had been seen going into a car, most of us thought that she must be with someone she knows because she wouldn't go into a car with a stranger. There were no reports of her being taken against her will and, as far as we were told, she had gone into the car cheerfully.'

Many who arrived later already knew otherwise, people such as John Rogers, who had seen the 'abduction' reference on social media. Some, who were out searching in the town, didn't know that fact. Many of those on Bryn y Gog that night say that even after the fact she'd been taken was established, they still didn't think the worst. For them there was a process of coping with what was unfolding in front of them, which didn't allow them to think too far ahead as to what could have happened. Each individual dealt with the unfolding story as best they could within themselves, taking in what they could see and hear others around them reacting as a part of that process. They were all very much in the moment. There was no room for thinking about possible scenarios and eventualities. All energy and focus was in the task at hand.

'There was only one thing on our mind,' a neighbour to the Jones family says, 'and that was finding April. Nothing else mattered.'

While all this was happening, in the nearby hamlet of Ceinws, a neighbour saw Mark Bridger reversing his vehicle into his drive an hour and five minutes after the 999 call. She was unable to tell if there was anyone else in the car, but with April being only five years old and small for her age, it would not have been easy to see her on a dark October evening.

Back in the town, Gareth Jones, a man in his mid-40s was working on his laptop at home when he heard a knock on his front window. He got up to see who was there and saw two women he knew. Instantly he thought they were there to collect money for some cause or other and thought that they had chosen a really dreadful night to do such a thing because the weather was so bad. The look on their faces soon convinced him otherwise.

'You haven't seen a little girl have you?'

'She was out on her bike and she's gone missing.'

'It's Coral's daughter.'

Fragments of the story unfolded on that doorstep in the same way as on dozens of other doorsteps at the same time. Some knew the family, some didn't. Gareth Jones had known Coral for some years. He didn't know April, as he says he had no reason to. He went back into the house to get his coat and a torch and onto the streets to help in the search, the two women continuing to raise awareness from door to door.

'I was under the distinct impression then that she had just got lost, as little girls sometimes do,' he says.

Gareth Jones was the mayor of Machynlleth at that time, but his initial response to the event was as a friend of the family and a concerned neighbour, not in any official capacity. The time for that would come later.

'It didn't matter that we thought that April was "only missing". That was no way to dismiss the situation. As far as we were concerned, one of the town's children wasn't where she was supposed to be, at home with her mum and dad, and we needed to go out to help look for her. As I was walking the streets, I was coming across more and more people who were doing the same. It was a strange feeling to see whichever corner you turned or whichever street you looked down, individuals, couples, small groups of people, all with torches in hand, weaving through the town's narrow streets, looking for April.'

That one sight, the overwhelming response among the townspeople, is mentioned by all who were out that night. It was also the experience of local shop owner, Alyson Jones.

'I was at home on the Monday evening, and I happened to see a reference to April having gone missing on Facebook. I had just made tea for my husband, who's disabled, and I turned to him and said that I just had to go out to look for her. I took the dog with me and a torch and went along the footpath at the back of the Plas near the gardens. I probably wouldn't venture there normally, in the dark, but it felt like the right thing to do that night. As I turned a corner, I will never forget what I saw. At every point, as I looked from right to left and back again, torchlight dotted the night sky; yellow/white circles flitting about like fluorescent moths. Some were in large clusters of more than one torch, maybe two or three here, one on its own there, five or six in another direction. It was an amazing pattern in the darkness and it made me feel amazed really that so many people had turned out. I was not alone after all.'

Alyson had seen April on Saturday afternoon. She runs Losin Lush, a sweet shop in the middle of Machynlleth, *losin* being the Welsh word for sweets. As Alison was about to close for the day, a few minutes before five o'clock, April came in with her mother and brother.

'You're never sure how to react when people come in just as you're about to close because it can be an irritation but, then again, they are customers. On seeing it was April and her family, it was no bother at all to welcome them, they were a lovely family who were regulars at Losin Lush. They had come in to buy sweets for the family for the weekend. They wanted a pound's worth of sweets for each of the five of them. April was keen to choose her favourite sweets, the ones she always had in my shop, the blue bonbons. Then a bag each was bought for her brother, sister, mum and dad. She left my shop a very happy child, in fact, as she always was anyway. That image of her leaving my shop the previous Saturday was what was in my mind when I learned that she was lost and when I stepped out to search for her.'

Each one of those out looking for April, as they left their homes, thought that they were the only ones; they, as many said in so many words, had just 'popped out to help'. But in reality, a large percentage of the population of the town had 'popped out to help' that dismal October evening.

At the same time as the search was intensifying, text messages were being sent by the dozen, hastily, frantically sent to whomever the sender thought might be able to help in any way possible. And, just as quickly, Facebook messages were distributed, social network cries for help, virtual pleas in a very real situation. From the very first few minutes of knowing that something was wrong, therefore, social network played its part. Its role was to increase significantly as the story unfolded.

Back on the streets of Machynlleth, Gareth Jones was now in a large throng of people who were walking briskly towards Huw Lewis Tyres at the top end of town, between Bryn y Gog and the town's famous clock tower. When they got there, a large crowd had already gathered to help in the search for April. At that time she was still only considered missing. The police asked the crowd to move down to the Leisure Centre where, again, others were gathering. Not far from the tyre depot, word had got through to people in the town's Bowling Club that a local girl was missing. They decided to do something to help as well. They put their drinks down and formed a group to go out searching themselves. These individual group searches happened at other centres dotted around the area.

Very quickly, through the use of more traditional methods, such as door-to-door knocking, and the use of contemporary social media, the word was spreading wider that April Jones was missing from her home on the Bryn y Gog estate.

One minibus full of young men heard the news on the radio. They were travelling from Llanelli to north Wales, and were on a drug rehabilitation scheme and on their way to a weekend of recreation and therapy. The leader of the organisation responsible for their rehab, Choose Life, is Alan Andrews.

'We were on our way up north and we heard the story of a missing five-year-old. We immediately stopped at the nearest petrol station and bought some flowers. We stopped when we got to Machynlleth and put them outside the Leisure Centre. I think we were the first to put flowers there. From my point of view, it was an opportunity to quietly make the point to those with me that, however low they had fallen, there was always someone in a worse situation than them. Getting them to imagine how April's parents felt was not difficult.'

After a while Kathleen Rogers walked into the town centre

with the group of people who initially congregated at the Bryn y Gog estate. At the Leisure Centre they were met by hundreds more who had gathered at the place where April had her swimming lesson just a few hours' earlier. It was also just over an hour and a half since she'd gone missing. An image on the Leisure Centre's foyer CCTV of April playing with her friend would prove to be the last image of her alive.

'I was totally overwhelmed by the sight that greeted me at the Leisure Centre,' Kathleen Rogers says. 'People were coming from everywhere. It was, in one way of looking at it, completely weird. Certainly it's difficult to explain to someone who wasn't there. There was such energy there, such a focus on finding April. It had obviously caught people's hearts in a remarkable way. I've certainly not felt a mass response of this kind in any other context before.'

As at Bryn y Gog, order seemed to establish itself among the large, thrown-together crowd. Local individuals areas of expertise were identified and railway workers, for example, who knew the area because of their day-to-day work and had the relevant maps, would take one group of people out to search. Members of the Dyfi Valley Motor Club played a key part in trying to coordinate the volunteers. Their knowledge of the area, especially of the off-road and forested areas, was invaluable. Likewise cyclists and, of course, farmers who had knowledge and quad bikes to help the process.

When John Rogers arrived at the Leisure Centre, his expertise was once again called upon. As part of his training and experience with Network Rail, he knew about crowd control issues, including controlling the scene of an incident and evacuating hundreds of people. He was one of those involved in coordinating the crowd into groups to go and search for April.

'Once that was done, I went off with four Arriva Trains workers in a van and spent all night driving through mostly the forested areas, round the back of places such as Furnace and Tre'r Ddôl, using our knowledge of the area, and the maps we used for work, to guide us. That first night, I went home for about an hour to get some sleep and change, and then back out.'

Along the many rivers in the Dyfi Valley, experienced anglers were using their knowledge to search the intricate pattern of waterways and riverbanks. Side-by-side with these fishermen, the area's poachers were also helping, having been given a temporary unofficial amnesty. Their knowledge of the rivers and streams, their banks and hiding places were more in need that night than the strict observance of any law enforcement.

As the week went on, local people with specialised knowledge or experience would assume a leadership role over the spontaneous groups of volunteers which turned up daily to help with the search. But a far more formal structure was soon in place, with the relevant emergency and rescue services in the early stages of coordinating what was to become the biggest police search in British history. But John Rogers's or the police's experience of crowd control was never called upon, however large the crowd of volunteers grew in those early days.

When the first of the many rescue teams arrived at the Leisure Centre, they too could not believe what they saw. Mark Jones from Brecon Mountain Rescue team was the first to be contacted by Dyfed Powys Police when they realised they would need specialist help.

'When I got to Machynlleth, and to the centre, it really was unbelievable to see hundreds of people outside in the dark and the rain. We certainly weren't used to seeing that, no way. It was difficult to know how to deal with it, at first. We might well be used to being called out to all sorts of rescues that are complex and dangerous. But usually it's just us and we are in total control. It soon became evident that we would need to devise a strategy to deal with what was needed to be done and to deal with what we faced when we got there.'

Late on Monday night, the owner of Read's Garage and Petrol Station, Nerys Zjalic, who knew April's family, received a phone call at home, asking her to open her garage for business again.

'I had a call explaining what was happening and asking if I would unlock the petrol station so that people from the area who were volunteering to look for April could get some petrol for the search. So, at about 11.30 p.m., I opened the garage again. Loads of people helped that night, it was quite a feeling to see how people had pulled together to search for one of the children from the town who had gone missing. The vast majority were local of course, but as the night wore on, people started to arrive from a far broader area.'

Texting and Facebook were beginning to come into their own now, having the effect hoped for by the army of message senders. The call for help was being pushed further and further afield. Word was getting out about a five-year-old from Machynlleth who couldn't be found, much further than the Dyfi Valley and indeed the rest of Wales. Countries outside the UK were also beginning to send in messages of support and hope.

As the night progressed, rumour spread that it might not be a case of a little girl gone missing. The possibility that she had been abducted began to be mentioned by those arriving from Bryn y Gog and Huw Lewis Tyres. The crowd gathering at the Leisure Centre were learning of this new development and, like a dark shadow, that unwelcome message worked its way around the crowd, rapidly filling the main hall at the Leisure Centre. The focus was changing. The mood was changing. People were beginning to feel that a community initially pulling together to look for a lost child was there now as the result of something more sinister. As one local farmer says, 'It was as if someone had grabbed you in the pit of your stomach, leaving a heavy weight behind.'

Once that message was out, the number of volunteers increased significantly. The pubs in the town emptied, as did the Indian restaurant.

'In a small town like this, nearly everybody is out looking

for her,' said restaurant owner Razul Islam at the time. 'It has shocked a small community like ours; we can't believe that such a thing can happen in a place like this.'

Before dawn the next day, nearly 30 miles of the area around the town had been searched. In one of the dozens of vehicles winding their way through the maze of country lanes and B-roads, were Kathleen Rogers and three others.

'Myself, my son's girlfriend and her mother all got into her car and headed towards some of the villages near Staylittle, known as Penfforddlas in Welsh and as Y Stay locally. It's in the hills, in the upland basin of the River Clywedog, near the reservoir of the same name. We went down tiny little roads we absolutely wouldn't dream of going down in any other circumstance. It was pitch-black, with no street lighting of any sort. I, for one, wouldn't drive round such remote, rugged an area in the day, never mind at two in the morning. And I certainly wouldn't stop the car and get out walking through the fields as we did that night.

'It was an amazing sight to see dozens of cars winding their way through those lanes and tracks. Now and again we were passed by a police Land Rover out on the same mission. They so understood what we were doing. It probably all looked chaotic, but we were all looking in different places. We didn't get in each other's way as you would have expected. We stayed out until about four in the morning.'

Farmers had brought out their quad bikes to cover difficult terrain, 4x4s were used and any other vehicle available and deemed useable. But many just walked and walked through terrain that can, at best, be described as difficult. Dense bracken, rivers with treacherous currents, river plains, jagged rocks, mountains and hills, thick forest and acres of rugged land, were all within touching distance of each other, all likely to be encountered by any one of the groups out searching.

Three pictures of April were released for circulation within hours – one of her in a long pink dress, one in an orange dress standing next to an unidentified friend, and the third quickly became the iconic photograph that soon captured everyone's heart. She's wearing that same orange dress, turning to her right towards the camera, showing a colourful butterfly tattoo on the top of her right arm. Her wistful, upward look at the camera, full of childhood innocence, is both heart-warming and engaging. It was an image that found its way right into the heart of public consciousness.

Many of those who had searched for hours into the small hours of Tuesday morning, then took time off work on the Tuesday to go back to help with the search in daylight hours. Some took the Wednesday off as well.

'There just wasn't any questioning the decision at all,' says Susan Williams (whose name has been changed) from Machynlleth, who works in the public sector in Aberystwyth. 'I phoned in sick on those days, well, there was no way of booking time-off through the proper channels, but also no way I was not going to help. I think people might have guessed where I actually was. There was always a risk of me being seen on TV anyway. None of that mattered. I don't think that my employers would have been bothered either, because of the nature of the story. They probably did turn a blind eye anyway, knowing exactly where I was.'

Gareth Jones joined a team of about ten volunteers, one of whom, another Gareth, was a keen golfer. They headed therefore to Machynlleth Golf Club, where his knowledge of the fairways would be best used. They had a vast area to search, of mixed terrain, including a lake at the top end. It was dark. It was still raining heavily. But they carried on for some hours, walking side-by-side in a line, covering every inch of the course and calling April's name out loud as they went. At one point, one of the others turned to Gareth, with a cold look of fear on his face. 'I hope to God I find her. But on the other hand, it's just really hit me now, I don't know what on the earth I would do if I did.'

The assumption had always been, in every heart and mind

out searching the area, that they were looking for a lost little girl, who would be found, confused and bewildered, but alive and well. Any suggestion to the contrary was an alien interruption to the work at hand and instantly dismissed. Such thoughts as the one articulated on the golf course might well have flashed through the minds of the other searchers, in other places, at some time or other during the long searching hours. But for that group on the golf course, one in their midst speaking such thoughts out loud – allowing for the possibility of such fear – threw them into a deep, contemplative silence. Many other individuals from the area now look back at that time of searching as a time of fighting such questions, trying to push them to the far corners of their thoughts; a time when hope and fear wrestled for position in their hearts and minds.

The social networks were really at full force within hours of the search beginning. By the early hours of the morning of 2 October, Twitter and Facebook were major players in the April Jones story. The little girl's name gathered momentum on Twitter, along with the hashtag FindApril. By 7 a.m. both were trending across the UK, along with the word Machynlleth. It soon passed all other topics that might have attracted the attention of the people of Britain. Hundreds of people had signed up to the Facebook page, many had downloaded the photos of April released by the police and posted them on their own personal pages. The grief, the concern and the care had gone highly public. Initially, it was those who were strangers to April and her family who were getting involved; now, strangers to the town of Machynlleth were responding in whichever way they thought appropriate. Those nearby were turning up to help in the search. Those further afield were posting messages of support and solidarity on Facebook and other social media platforms.

When the army of volunteers who had been out most of the night returned to the Leisure Centre at about 4 a.m., the various convoys would report where they had been for the previous four hours or so. At that early hour, having been out searching for April in terrible weather and conditions, most of the volunteer searchers went home to grab a few hours' much-needed sleep. But after only two hours' rest, they were back at the Leisure Centre by 6 a.m.

'By the time I got back there at six, the police were fully in control then and it had taken on the form of a proper structured investigation,' Kathleen Rogers recalls. 'But even though that was the case, the unofficial groups – if we can call them that – were also still very much in action. So the two were working side-by-side.'

The police had launched their search at a very stage on the evening of October the first. Their efforts gathered momentum quickly as the evening turned to night. Soon, there were many officers, police dogs and specialist teams out looking for her, working alongside the hundreds of volunteers. It was, for that reason, an unusual police operation as well.

By midday on 2 October, offers of support from other forces started to flood in to Dyfed Powys Police. Soon, many other police forces were involved, including British Transport Police. Mountain rescue units from different areas throughout Wales and England were called upon or offered their services, as did cave rescue teams. Every fire service in Wales sent members to the search.

Also among the army of volunteers on hand that day were workers in various jobs who'd been given permission to be part of the operation. Powys County Council announced that refuse and recycling collections were suspended for the day, so that the binmen could help in the search. The Royal Mail gave specific instructions to all their postmen and women in the area to be on the lookout for the little girl as they travelled through the area. Railway workers too had similar instructions as the mid Wales trains made their way through the landscape of Dyfi Valley and beyond. Farmers searched their fields and outhouses as they went about their daily tasks.

By tea-time on that first full day since April had gone

missing, the police announced that they had made an arrest. A 46-year-old man was in police custody being questioned on suspicion of being involved in April's disappearance. The police also confirmed that the man had been arrested while walking in the area with his dog, and that a vehicle had been compounded as well. It was confirmed that it was information from the public that had led to the arrest of the man. The message that a man was in custody so soon after her disappearance raised hopes of April being alive, and that the man would reveal her whereabouts.

But at the same time, other feelings were also churning in the stomachs of those who had been out looking for April. The detained man was local. He was one of them. They knew him. At that stage, however, such thoughts were occasional visitors, kept in their place by the more proactive thoughts of finding the child. Hope was more dominant at that point in the week. One thing was clear, in a timespan of less than 24 hours, the residents of a small market town in mid Wales had experienced two or three different episodes of deep-seated emotions. Even though they were a people who shared the same space in a tiny corner of mid Wales, they certainly had not been through such collective mass emotions ever before.

Whatever the nature of the volunteering, whatever the contribution, there was unity. The overriding emotion was deep-rooted compulsion, a strong sense of determination and hope. So the search continued. Emergency services and volunteers alike, experts and amateurs, professionals and well-wishers, side-by-side in their quest to find April. But this was now an official police operation as well. It was an abduction. An arrest had been made. The Leisure Centre took on a more formal role in the police inquiry, as did Y Plas mansion next door. When this happened, some of the townspeople used some of the other clubs and buildings in the town as well, as makeshift headquarters from which they could coordinate their activities, the Bowls Club being one such place. The nature of the volunteers' work was changing as the week went on. What they were allowed to do, and what they were able to do, was changing. Only four days into the search, the town had to face yet another twist in its tragic tale.

3

A tragic twist, a change of plan

THE RELATIONSHIP BETWEEN the hundreds of volunteers from far and wide and the police, search and rescue professionals and other emergency services was, from the start, a difficult one. Not that such a situation was down to antagonism or any form of disagreement. It was purely because the situation was unprecedented. No-one knew beforehand what the correct procedure was. Such a large team of rescue and emergency professionals had never come face-to-face with a spontaneous gathering of local and not-so-local volunteers before. There was no manual to turn to, no more than there was a manual to help the people of Machynlleth deal with what they were confronted with on that first day of October. So how did both groups work side-by-side? They certainly tried their best to find a way to cooperate, because they had a common goal. The professional searchers certainly didn't want to quash the spirit of the genuine and sincere friends, family and community members who had given up days of their time to look for April. They knew that would be cruel, destructive and, on another level, counterproductive. They didn't need the antagonism which might result from a rejection of their help among the grieving people of Machynlleth.

But there were also operational issues. An enthusiastic, but unregulated, army of local volunteers was difficult to contain and coordinate within a structured search and rescue operation. For the first two-and-a-half full days of the operation both searched side-by-side.

But by the time Thursday came, things had to change.

45

Bridger had been in custody in Aberystwyth since Tuesday. Unofficially, the growing belief within the emergency and rescue services was that he had actually killed April. This led to an understandable dilemma. There had to be a difference between what was said publicly and what was believed in private.

'It was a very awkward time,' says Mark Jones of the Brecon Mountain Rescue service. 'I was telling the guys in my team that we were, by then, looking for a body, while at the same time not saying that to the public involved so sincerely. It was a difficult thing to deal with in terms of man-management, if nothing else. Personally, of course, it was even more difficult than that.'

A change of approach was needed. On Thursday Dyfed Powys Police, who were leading the investigation, called a meeting of the lead investigating officers, rescue services and community leaders from the town. The Rev. Kathleen Rogers and town mayor, Gareth Jones, were at that meeting.

'We were called to a meeting in Y Plas with the lead investigators,' recalls Kathleen Rogers. 'There we were told that the police now saw this as a murder investigation, which changed everybody's outlook on the whole sorry story. It was a difficult meeting to say the least, but not half as difficult as what was to face us immediately after.'

Once the relevant leaders met and discussed the developments, the news had to be shared with the people using Y Plas as their headquarters. Kathleen Rogers took her place alongside Dyfed Powys Police's criminal investigation team on a makeshift stage in Y Plas's hall. The police carefully explained that the time had now come for the volunteers to step aside and leave the searching to those trained to do so. Why? Because it was now a murder enquiry. A little girl gone missing had become an abduction – and now there was horrific news of her suspected murder.

'I will never forget the reaction amongst the hundreds gathered that evening,' recalls Kathleen Rogers. 'It was an atmosphere I had certainly never experienced before and I find it extremely difficult to describe it even now. How do you describe such a heavy silence? Those of us on the stage were there for a long time before proceedings began, as it were, but even then no-one in the big hall of Y Plas said a word. It was an atmosphere heavy with significance and meaning, a deep-rooted poignancy, a knowing without being told, an understanding without information. Silence has never been so significant and meaningful to me.'

And then, one of the police officers leading the investigation called Kathleen Rogers forward to address those in the hall. She froze. She wondered what on the earth she could say. No theological training, no prior experience in her former profession as a nurse, could have prepared her to face addressing a hall full of Machynlleth people about the abduction of a five-year-old girl.

'One question went through my head, round and round again – "What do I say? What do I say? What do I say?" – for what seemed like an eternity. I looked round at the sea of faces before me and wondered what on the earth I could say to these people. We shared the same town. We had lived the same tragedy for the previous three-and-a-bit days. What words did I have that would mean anything to them? I felt that all their eyes were staring at me – not in a horrible way, burning a hole in the back of my head – but a needy staring, a looking for some comforting words, an expectant gaze that wanted to be met by reassuring words. They were looking for something, and in my direction. It was so sad, so poignant.'

To this day, Kathleen Rogers cannot remember what she said at that meeting. She does remember praying with her fellow townspeople, but cannot remember the content of the prayer. Speaking about that meeting today still proves to be difficult for her.

On the way out of that emotionally-charged meeting, the media were there waiting to get any information they could. Fresh from having to deal with standing before her fellow

Machynlleth people, she now had TV cameras in her face. If she didn't know what to say to her own people, she certainly didn't know what to say to the newshounds in front of her at the end of that meeting.

'The cameras were like ants all around us. There were myriad microphones in my face all the time. Luckily, my son was by my side all the time looking after me. He told me to walk away from them. But, as much as I appreciated his care and concern for me, I knew that by that Thursday, my role meant it wasn't that easy to just walk away. I had a public role thrust upon me.'

She answered questions as best as she could. Then someone she recognised from the TV, but whose name she can't remember, asked her a question.

'He asked me, "How do people feel about this then?". I just turned to look at him, with one definite thought inside my mind – how the hell do you think they feel? I came that close to actually saying that to him! I couldn't believe I was asked such a question at such a time.'

What hit everyone really hard that evening at Y Plas was the realisation that they were not going to find April alive. Almost continual searching for her, night and day, across every inch of local terrain, had now come down to the cold fact that this was a murder investigation. Many said it was on hearing that one word, 'murder', that their hearts sank, that they felt completely hopeless after days of living on nothing but hope. That was what made the silence so heavy in that Thursday meeting. A town was now beginning coming to terms with what had happened in their midst.

Not everyone could accept that though. There were many who thought that the fact that a body hadn't been found was both an indication that the police had got it wrong and that there actually was still hope that she could be found alive.

'I just couldn't believe it,' one mother from an outlying village said, 'that there was a murder charge without a body. It just didn't make sense. If that was the case, why hasn't the Madeleine McCann story been treated like a murder investigation, because her body hasn't been found? It hasn't, even six years later. It's still a missing little girl story. So why can't April's be the same? Why is this one murder?'

The sense of frustration and lack of acceptance at what they had been told was tangible to many. Some rationalised it in a similar way to the lady who saw comparisons with Madeleine McCann's story: no body being an obvious indicator that there might not actually be a murder case to answer. Others had different justifications, but were no less dogmatic.

'It doesn't make sense at all,' said one man from the town centre, 'How can it be murder if there's no body? It just doesn't make sense.'

'We're not going to buy this murder argument, no way,' said another mother from a neighbouring village. 'We'll keep going until we find a body. That's it, end of.'

Mayor Gareth Jones accepted that they were now faced with having to deal with the murder of one of the town's children. He accepted that the police had enough evidence, or could rely on enough information to accept that Bridger was guilty of taking April's life. He also realised on that Thursday why the police were so insistent that the volunteering public needed to step down and let the professionals take over.

'It wasn't said in so many words at all, but the obvious inference was that the police didn't want the public to be in the situation where they might actually find a body. That would be too much for any of us to deal with.'

That brought Gareth Jones right back to the comment made by his namesake while they were out searching on the golf course on that first Monday. What would they actually do if they found April? The police were obviously anxious to avoid any member of the searching public facing such a stark reality. That thought became especially poignant when it was realised that many of the volunteers had taken their children with them to search.

Not only did the public have to deal with this new

development, but the rescue teams had to as well. Mark Jones from Brecon Mountain Rescue has mentioned dealing with knowing that it was a murder case before the public knew. He also was aware of another effect on the public involvement in the search.

'Apart from the obvious trauma which would have happened if one of the searchers had come across a body, and that was very real indeed, there was also the issue of a team of local volunteers coming across a body and, unknowingly and innocently enough, contaminating the crime scene by their very presence. Vital evidence might have been unwittingly disturbed. It made so much sense to stand the volunteers down, even if not everyone understood why that was done.'

That approach might well have been fairly straightforward when it came to dealing with the public. But Mark Jones also had to deal with members of his own team.

'I had over a hundred people in my charge,' he explains, 'and one morning I called them all together and spoke to them about how I saw things. I gave each and every one of them the option to bring their time searching for April to an end, and to go back home. I said that they were all responsible individuals and no-one would think any the less of them if they were to decide to leave the search there and then and go home. There would be no criticism. In fact, far from it. They had done more than their duty already in extremely difficult circumstances in terms of both terrain and weather. Many of the group, of course, were parents themselves and who knows how distressing that could have been for them if they had come across April. It could have stayed with them for the rest of their lives. Others, of course, were grandparents, uncles, aunts, brothers and sisters.'

But not one member of his team accepted the offer to go home. Rescue workers spoken to said that there were many factors that influenced the decision to stay. The obvious one was the fact that they were looking for a five-year-old girl and they were thinking of her family and the trauma they must be going through.

Another reason they said they stayed was the overwhelming sense of goodwill and supportive spirit they encountered from volunteers in the town. The shift times spent out searching for miles and miles around the town were long, with many staying out for up to 22 hours at a time.

'The combination of the reason for the search, the highly-charged collective spirit at the Leisure Centre and Y Plas, the weather, the rugged territory we had to work in, the long shifts – it all made for a very emotional environment. Usually, we can keep emotions in check and get on with the job. It wasn't like that this time and there were many occasions when it proved totally impossible. It was always a real comfort to return to the Leisure Centre after being out searching, and seeing that there was plenty of food there for us whatever time of day or night we got back. It was good, proper food as well. More than that though were the warm smiles and friendly welcome from the volunteers helping with the catering. After what might well have been a harrowing stint out looking, they certainly nursed us back to some kind of normality. It was, unquestioningly, an extremely supportive environment, crucial in such circumstances and very rare.'

The rescuers, of course, were out for hours on end and would come across many people who lived in the countryside. When they had to walk across farmland, they didn't ask permission from farmers beforehand. That would have added significantly to their day and they assumed that everyone knew what they were doing and would be supportive of that. But some of the rescue teams were taken by surprise by the locals' attitude. One farmer's story sums that up, as he recalls looking out of his window and seeing a team in the fields below his farmhouse.

'I opened the front door and stood in the doorway shouting across to them. They stopped in their tracks and looked across at me, obviously uncertain about why I was there and what I was shouting. One of them told me later that when they heard me shout and they looked up, seeing me in the doorway and filling it with my big frame, they feared the worst. In their experience on other searches up until then, they would expect confrontation of some sort, and quite often outright antagonism. They were hugely relieved to understand that what I shouted at them was, "Tea or coffee boys?".'

Many Machynlleth residents shared similar stories of conversations with members of the emergency services. Residents at an elderly care home in the town, for example, feeling they needed to contribute but who couldn't join in like everyone else, took to baking cakes for the rescue teams. A good relationship built up between them, a relationship of trust and co-dependency. The same could be said of the police presence on the Bryn y Gog estate in those early days in the first week of October.

'That first week,' a mother who lives on the estate remembers, 'it was totally heart-wrenching. The police presence was obvious every hour of the day as they either stood guard, as it were, searched, went from door to door or just called back and forth to Coral and Paul's house. You'd see them as you closed your curtains of an evening and they were still there when you opened the curtains in the morning.'

Then, suddenly, everything changed.

'Every cordon, every policeman, disappeared overnight! I got up one morning and when I opened the curtains this time, the whole estate was clear of any police presence. They had obviously scaled down their operation on Bryn y Gog during the night when we were all in bed. I suppose that was less disruptive for us, and we get that. But, the overwhelming feeling was "Oh my God, we're on our own now!" For the first time since April disappeared, we felt vulnerable, isolated. That was the point that we realised how safe we felt while they were there. But we didn't think of it as a safety blanket at the time. In fact, it was an inconvenience in a way because we had to duck under police tape to walk out of our houses and our cars couldn't be moved. But we realised when the police had gone how OK it was to be at home while they were roaming the estate. The fact they had gone was horrible, it was terrifying. It was as if nothing had happened, but it had.'

The police withdrawal from Bryn y Gog gave the residents there one very clear, stark message too. It had already been announced that Mark Bridger had been arrested. Therefore, when they withdrew, the people of Bryn y Gog thought immediately that the police had gathered all the evidence needed and that he was probably responsible for April's death.

With the public search having come to an end, it did not mean that that was the end of the public's endeavours for April. The same energy, the same sympathy, the same drive was still in every heart and mind as it had been from the very first minute they heard of the abduction. But new ways were needed now to deal with the situation. And that new way was through donating food to feed rescuers and police. The donations increased significantly as the week went by, especially when residents could no longer search for April themselves.

On the Friday, Alyson Jones, from Losin Lush, decided that she needed to contribute something to help. She had a very close relationship with the primary school – the school even had a version of her shop where children would learn to count through the sale of sweets in the school's shop. That's how Alyson came to know April when she was in the nursery class in the school. So Alyson opened the shop on the Friday as normal and set about a task.

'I started to put together bags of sweets to take to the school, having phoned the school first to see how many were there that day. I eventually put together 250 bags of sweets, blue bonbons in particular, which April had bought the Saturday before. I then took them up to the school and distributed them to every child.

'On my return, I had a phone call from one of my suppliers, asking if I wanted to place my usual order. I said I needed double that day. Because that was so unusual and such a large amount, they asked why. I explained about the delivery I'd made to the school and they said that I could have my entire order for free.'

That kind of support was not unusual. In the above example, the fact it was from a company outside the area made it a little different but, in principle, the support from all around was overwhelming. Many volunteers set to work identifying the things that were needed, where they could be obtained and how they could be best distributed.

Food for the police, fire and rescue teams arrived from everywhere. And it wasn't just big bags of everything, but boxes full. The supermarkets in the area, Morrisons and the Co-op, sent regular daily provisions, as did the market traders who visited the town every Wednesday, many of them coming from south Wales and the Midlands as well as the local area. 'They were magnificent' seems to have been the common description of the way the travelling traders supported the town. On the first Wednesday after April Jones was taken, the majority of traders stayed away, saying that they didn't want to disturb the community at such a sensitive time. They returned the following week to play their part in the search for April. Smaller independent traders, such as William Lloyd Williams MBE, the butcher in town, played their part from day one.

'Everybody just did what we felt was instinctively the right thing to do,' says Will Lloyd, who famously accepted his honour from the Queen at Buckingham Palace with his usual ballpoint pen tucked behind his ear.

But when the volunteers' attention turned towards supplying provisions, it became apparent that so much more than food was needed.

'One early need that was identified,' says Kathleen Rogers, 'was for deodorants or antiperspirants for the police, fire and rescue teams. Those out searching in the wilds and in the rivers, or those doing the door-to-door enquiries, were in desperate need of such things after being out for so long. Word was sent out that's what was needed and, within hours, there were boxes of all sorts of deodorants and antiperspirants arriving at the Leisure Centre. But not only these things, soaps of various kinds came as well, hairspray and other hair products, along with shower gels, shampoos and towels. There was even one box of hair colour sent by someone, for some reason. They mostly came from the broader Machynlleth area, but a lot of stuff came from towns in north and south Wales as well. I remember there was a donation of food from Waitrose and we haven't got one of those anywhere near us here. There were also plentiful supplies of men's and women's underwear and socks. Basically, whatever was needed to make the lives of the hundreds of rescuers of various kinds as bearable and comfortable as possible during such difficult times.'

With such a fantastic response to the request for food, there was now the need for it to be prepared and cooked. Teams of people were organised to deal with the food, rotas drawn up for each hour of the day. Meals were initially prepared at the Leisure Centre, but then operations moved to the small kitchen at Y Plas, and the cafeteria of the Leisure Centre was used for storage of boxed food. It was full from floor to ceiling almost permanently. There was so much food, in fact, that extra fridges were required to store it. A request was sent out for them and within a short space of time, two brand new fridges were delivered free of charge by generous donors.

Many rescue workers and local people alike testify to the extreme pride with which the catering volunteers went about their work, summed up by one story in particular.

'I remember being at the Leisure Centre,' says one local man, 'and I saw some of the policemen get up from their table and start to gather their plates and cups to take them back to the kitchen. Some of those helping there at the time rushed up to them and told them quite clearly that no way were they supposed to do that and they were to put everything back on the table immediately! It wasn't an anger of any sort, just a strong sense that that's why they were there, to help, to free the police up from any menial tasks so that they could just get on with the work they were really there to do. It was really quite caring in its own way.'

Some of those volunteering with food preparation also got involved with another activity which increased in momentum as that first week progressed – fundraising. Many chose to concentrate their efforts solely on raising money for the newly-established April Jones Fund. This involved collection buckets throughout town and selling pink ribbons. The pink ribbon, a fully-tied ribbon, not the pink ribbon loop used by a breast cancer charity, became the symbol of the search. It was a very simple, visible symbol that was instantly identifiable with April Jones, pink being her favourite colour. That's why her mother Coral had initiated the ribbon campaign. It was, however, to become a symbol of much debate, as much as, initially, a symbol of hope, as will be explained later.

By that first Friday in October, the good people of Machynlleth had changed the direction of their focus. The efforts to look for a little girl lost had turned into a full-scale search for an abducted child, which then, a few days' later turned into a murder investigation. These were psychological and emotional changes which affected everyone deeply in many different ways.

Unknown to most of the searchers, rescuers and volunteers, there was one notable person helping to make sandwiches – Coral, April's mum. She'd decided that she needed to help. It was one way in which she could keep busy and try to deal with the world that was crashing around her. But she was also overwhelmed by the response of the community, and felt she should be part of it. She took her place alongside all the others buttering and filling sandwiches. And she was allowed to just get on with it, as she had requested. During the times Coral did that, she was as one with the people of her own community, pulling together because a tragedy had shaken them to the core. Except in her case, the tragedy was the taking of her own daughter's life.

4

This small, quiet town

No-one but the Jones family can understand what they've been through since October 2012. It's futile for anyone to say, 'I know how you feel'. We don't. Only families such as the McCanns and the families of Holly Wells and Jessica Chapman get close. But even then, no two such stories are exactly the same. They all bring their own very personal tragedies, individual, indescribable and unfathomable nightmares.

But that said, the taking of April Jones's life did spark a huge public reaction as has already been outlined. It touched people everywhere in the UK and far beyond. But the most affected community was the town that was home to the family. Machynlleth was rocked to its core. The fabric of a small, traditional Welsh community was violently unpicked, unravelled and torn apart. Its people reacted before they really knew what they were reacting to. It was an instinctive response because they knew something was wrong even if they didn't know the details. They acted before they understood, because that was the natural thing for them to do in this traditional, quiet, mid Wales market town. So what kind of town is this Machynlleth?

Machynlleth lies in the hills of the Dyfi Valley, looking out on the magnificent Dyfi estuary. It is breathtakingly beautiful. It sits at the topmost western corner of the county of Powys. Over the centuries, Powys has been described as the Eden of Wales. Daniel Defoe, on his tour through Great Britain, was struck by the 'Welch horses' in many areas of the county, as well as the monuments and Roman camps. In more recent decades,

Powys has been called the paradise of Wales and 'a large world of small things'. Such natural and historical beauty still draws tourists to this day. But Machynlleth hasn't been invaded and turned into a tacky tourist town, unlike perhaps the kiss-me-quick-candy-floss culture of nearby seaside town, Tywyn.

Machynlleth is an anomaly. It would not have been a town known to many people outside Wales before last October. In the main, it's a small town, driven through by those on their way from north to south Wales or vice versa, somewhere to pass through or to stop for a coffee on the way to somewhere else. But, it's especially popular with cyclists and motorcyclists on a Sunday. For some decades, it's been famed as a destination for those who seek alternative sources of technology. The Centre for Alternative Technology perches high up on the edge of the town. Opened in 1973 in a disused slate quarry, it has established itself as a major British environmental centre.

Looking round Machynlleth today, with its two main streets forming a T where the famous clock tower stands, it's easy to see the colours that make up Machynlleth's palette. An eye's journey in and around it's old-new and new-old buildings shows that the town is a weave of threads; coarse wool, fine wool, cotton and the occasional silk. A 'carthen' (Welsh blanket) of a town.

Like every other town, it boasts a rich history, as Defoe saw centuries ago. But today it also has a centre for alternative healing; many antiques shops; a vegetarian café and one that tells you it's OK to breastfeed at its tables; two art galleries, one in an old chapel dedicated to modern art; a second-hand bookshop and a second-hand and brand new bookshop as well as the Coch y Bonddu bookshop for fishing and natural history reading material; two practitioners of skin art and body-piercing.

The stately and the quirky sit in each other's shadow – on the one hand, Y Plas mansion and gardens show clear signs of a gentrified landowner past, but on the other hand, down the road, a distressed piano stands in the front garden of a house on the main road, where plants grow through the keyboard and a plant-bearing acoustic guitar gently weeps in the gravel by its side.

There are buildings made of Machynlleth brick that offer street food and another offers collectables; a prize-winning butcher boasts of selling vegetarian meat; where a National Milk Bar used to be, is now an auction house, there's an Indian restaurant next door and up the road there's a pebble-windowed, fine dining restaurant.

You can buy an Aga near to the Red Lion that sells lager; there are two places to buy rolls of cloth and pins; there's rainbow clothing on roadside racks, with cutlery clocks looking on while a window full of crockery begs people to part with money to help neglected pets.

You can enjoy a pint of Celt with a pigeon in an old coaching house which the *Sunday Times* once proclaimed made the best pizzas in the UK; an emporium sells fine jewellery not far from Dick's chips which is across the road from Spar. The Job Centre next door is one of the busiest places in town, but the bakery has closed down; buildings of slate prop up inns that slake the thirst; the newsagent breaks the story that a local man has won the UK Shed of The Year competition for a shed which has three-quarters of a rowing boat as a roof.

It's a round ball town in an oval ball nation; a plaque high up pays tribute to man from the town who pitched a baseball for the Boston Beaneaters and led the National League for pitching percentages in 1896; on the perforated periphery of this postage stamp town centre, there's petrol, cars for sale, a cottage hospital, building supplies, a railway station and another chippy.

In this land of centuries-old myth, fable and legend, one shop sells dragon droppings and it's a dragon that has two tongues as most of the shop windows show names and information in Welsh and English.

In one café, there are bottles of Heartsease mineral water for sale, locally sourced, and made from the Heartsease Poppy, a flower which, according to local tradition, has properties that can mend a broken heart. So timely, but if only.

In the public life of Wales today, however, Machynlleth doesn't play a particularly active part. But, a guidebook, *Welcome to Ardal Machynlleth*, available in one of the shops, says that Machynlleth is a town that has, over the last decade or so, begun to rediscover itself, to move out of its own shadow. It says that it's forming an identity for itself which is moving on from the no-man's-land it used to inhabit. At least, it was starting to do so.

Machynlleth used to play a far greater role in Welsh life. A few hundred yards from the town clock lies the site of the parliament buildings of Owain Glyndŵr, dated 1440. Glyndŵr was the Welsh leader who, seven centuries ago, succeeded in uniting more of the disparate tribal areas of Wales than had been possible until then. To rule this new, united Wales, he set up what was to be the first parliament for the Welsh in Machynlleth, centuries before the devolved Senedd in Cardiff Bay. Today, Glyndŵr's Senedd is an important tourist attraction.

The area's slate industry, as well as drovers and their cattle, made Machynlleth an important town in Wales. In later years, however, Machynlleth has had a lower profile, adjusting to the modern rhythms which have seen it nestle quietly into the Welsh shadows. But, one obvious exception to that in recent decades was the opening of the first ever Laura Ashley shop in the world, at 35 Maengwyn Street in the early 1960s. The building bears a plaque to note that fact, and that shop now deals in interior and artists' supplies. Laura Ashley and her family had moved to the area following a flooding incident in her English home. Her relocation to mid Wales was the beginning of her worldwide empire. Only Laura Ashley's name had ever given Machynlleth a place on the global map. Until now.

Life changed for Machynlleth on the day that April disappeared when people pulled together to look for her. Events came to a head on the following weekend. With Mark Bridger arrested on Tuesday and charged on Friday, Saturday was the first day in which the people of Machynlleth would wake up and begin to react to the depth of their feelings and how they'd deal with it. Their unity in grief was about to show itself in an emphatic way. And it would capture the hearts of those in far-flung countries who had no idea where Machynlleth was.

On the Saturday following April's disappearance, vicar Kathleen Rogers was reflecting on the service she would prepare for the next day. It was incomprehensible how things had changed in her parish since the previous Monday evening. The original plans for that first Sunday in October was a Eucharist service in each one of the four churches in her care, across Machynlleth and its hinterland. As the week's events unfolded, it became obvious that such an arrangement would not be possible, as she wouldn't be able to travel to all four churches while continuing with the role thrust upon her less than a week earlier. So all four congregations were called together to one bilingual service at St Peter's Church in Machynlleth. But even that would prove to be impossible to hold.

As the week drew to its close, people who normally didn't attend church began asking Kathleen Rogers if they could come to the service on Sunday.

Alyson, from Losin Lush, was one of those who had shown a desire to be at the service. She had no previous link with the church and was not of formal religion. On hearing further such requests, the vicar then began to wonder if others in the community would turn up for the same reasons on that Sunday.

'A friend told me that many of the elderly in the town felt that they couldn't contribute in any way, being too old to search. Some, of course, did bake cakes, and the like. But there were still many who felt left out, who felt helpless as they saw the town pull together. They felt isolated from this showing of goodwill and support. So some of them told my friend that they wanted to walk together to church on that Sunday morning. To make their stand, to share in the hope.'

61

Word then spread around the town that there would be a gathering on the Bryn y Gog estate on Sunday morning and that they would then be heading in procession to the town centre. As this news filtered through to Kathleen Rogers, she knew that the Sunday morning service would not be anything remotely like the usual service.

'There was no way that we could conduct a communion service with the number of people who were telling me that they were going to be in church that morning. I initially thought that we would revert to a morning prayer service. But it became apparent that that kind of service would be, quite simply, inappropriate. There was only one answer. We had to create a brand new service to respond to the events that had happened in our town during the week.'

It quickly became evident that that Sunday morning service would be a major community event. Help was needed in the structuring of it, in achieving the correct tone, the right spirit that would reach out and touch a diverse community in its grief. The Bishop of the Diocese of Bangor, the Right Reverend Andrew John, travelled to Machynlleth on Saturday to meet with Kathleen Rogers. Together they would coordinate what was to be the main community response to the taking of one of their own.

Since the Tuesday after April disappeared, Kathleen Rogers had seen her role as one of being there for the community – her parishioners in effect, even if many didn't attend her church. She felt a strong sense of that's how it should be. Paul and Coral were being given protection, comfort and support by the police family liaison officer, so Kathleen concentrated on the community. Her time to offer support to the parents would come later.

'We soon realised that we had to start from scratch with this service, and that's what we did. As late as the Saturday night, I phoned the parents of two children to ask if they were willing for their children to carry a candle and book in procession down through the church. Thankfully they agreed.'

When the Sunday morning came, the church was full, with people standing all around the perimeter. Outside the church, the grounds were full as well. The night before, somebody realised that people outside the building would need to hear what was going on. So speakers were hurriedly erected. Another example of personal initiative.

Another late Saturday request then landed at Kathleen's doorstep. Sky Television wanted to broadcast the service. Eventually, and not without great deal of discussion locally, it was agreed that they could, but only with restricted use of cameras. The service was also shown on the BBC.

Before the service began, Kathleen Rogers waited in the vestry. The Bishop of Bangor was with her, as were a few of her clerical colleagues who had come to give support to the community and Kathleen.

'I was extremely nervous before going on to begin the service. I was really worked up. At that point I hadn't, of course, seen how many were there. I'm not sure if knowing that beforehand would have helped or hindered. As it turned out, as soon as I walked in through the side door into the church, I felt all right. I could do what I knew needed to be done.'

A simple service had been carefully planned the night before to give some structure to a community's grief. Simple in its essence, its spirit and its intention. Its theme, readings and hymns would strike a chord with those not familiar with going to church regularly.

The opening hymn that Sunday morning was 'Morning Has Broken'. It's a relatively modern Christian song, and was composed in 1931. It also made the charts through a version by Cat Stevens in 1971. It's a popular hymn at children's services. It is sung to a Celtic tune which was also used for the lyrics of a child's Christmas carol, 'Child in the Manger, Infant of Mary'.

The Reverend Kathleen Rogers then stepped forward and read two poems. The first one, 'Mum', was specifically for Coral Jones, April's mum. It described a mother's attributes which had resonance with Coral. The second poem, 'There's a

Friend for Little Children', introduced a Christian theme of a heavenly refuge for children of all ages, but for young children specifically. It offered the hope that although April might be lost, she was not alone wherever she was because of a Friend that was always with her. The refrain, 'There's a home for little children,' offered comfort for those who sought it, that April was in a home, even if it wasn't the one in Bryn y Gog.

In the bilingual prayer that followed, Kathleen Rogers referred to the future as being dark and the present as being uncertain; she also mentioned taking courage from belief. The congregation then recited the Lord's Prayer in Welsh and English. The service reflected clearly its community. Given the option to recite the Lord's Prayer in either language, most did so in Welsh. In times of grief language is so much more than vocabulary.

The second hymn was, 'Lord, Make me an Instrument of your Peace'. This hymn is a Christian Catholic prayer and is often attributed to St Francis of Assisi. It is widely regarded as central to the devotion and faith of the church at large, and plays a central part in the story of people as diverse in politics and theology as Margaret Thatcher and Archbishop Desmond Tutu.

The peace in Machynlleth that morning was a fractious one. There was no animosity, no hostility, no warring factions, no conflict, but there was a crack in the fabric of the community. They needed the pieces to be at peace as they sought to understand what had fractured their lives.

Lord, make me an instrument of Your peace;
Where there is hatred, let me sow love;
Where there is injury, pardon;
Where there is doubt, faith;
Where there is despair, hope;
Where there is darkness, light;
Where there is sadness, joy.

O, Divine Master, Grant that I may not so much seek
To be consoled, as to console;
To be understood as to understand;
To be loved, as to love.
For it is in giving that we receive;
It is in pardoning that we are pardoned;
And it is in dying that we are born to eternal life.

A reading in Welsh then followed – the story of the Good Samaritan. A popular, well-known parable that could surely have had no more resonance anywhere than in Machynlleth that week. Certainly nobody passed by on the other side in that town, that first week of October.

The Bishop of Bangor then led those assembled in prayer. Those standing on the grass among the gravestones could hear everything, but could see nothing; they stood in reverential silence and respected devotion. After another Welsh reading, Kathleen Rogers led the congregation by reading Psalm 23, 'The Lord is my Shepherd'. In her soft, sympathetic voice that held back from being sentimental, the vicar's tone was reassuring as she referred to people being led through the Valley of the Shadow of Death.

The next hymn drew on an altogether different tradition, 'Guide Me O Thou Great Redeemer', could not be more Welsh in its provenance. Based on words written by the man deemed to be the greatest Welsh hymn writer, William Williams, the tune 'Cwm Rhondda' has been sung by many at diverse occasions: from the raucous anthem-singing of the Welsh rugby fan, the delicate rendition in the film *African Queen*, to the more stately interpretations in the funeral of both Diana, Princess of Wales, and the Queen Mother, as well as the wedding of William and Catherine. An integral part of Welsh identity, as well as a central part of the Welsh Christian tradition, the rendition of this hymn that morning was robust if not defiant, strong if not raucous. And always united.

The Bishop then addressed the congregation and said that

the church was a good place for them to be together, shoulder to shoulder. He mentioned that he was an outsider who had been deeply moved by the response in Machynlleth and he wanted to thank everyone for the compassion they had shown. There were many references to Paul and Coral and the way they had responded personally, and the way that the community had supported them.

As he spoke, the hundreds gathered outside stood linking arms or hand-in-hand. Most of those who chose to connect in that way were mothers and children. They heard Andrew John speak of the messages and donations that had come in from all over the world. He went on to say that the truth really was stronger than darkness and that was what was being seen in the town at that moment in time. He drew to a close by saying that the gift the community could give April was to extinguish despair.

He thanked the emergency and rescue services at length before handing over to Kathleen Rogers who introduced the most poignant part of the service. Two children, Lydia and Gwern, stood at the back of the church, one holding a candle for April and the other the Book of Hope opened in her name. They proceeded down the central aisle, each wearing a pink ribbon in April's memory. On arrival at the altar, Kathleen Rogers held the candle aloft while the Bishop blessed it.

The final hymn was 'All Things Bright and Beautiful', again associated with children's services. This was the hymn sung by the children of Pantglas Primary School, Aberfan, at their assembly on the morning of 21 October 1966, minutes before a sliding coal tip took the lives of 116 children and 28 adults. In Machynlleth on Sunday, 7 October 2012, it was announcing that hymn which finally broke Kathleen Rogers's resolve. She had held her emotions together throughout the service, but that hymn made her lose focus and control. Keeping her emotions in check was a battle.

'I don't know if it was because it was the end of the service and I realised that we had managed to get through everything, or what. But it was that final hymn that broke me in the end. It could well have been a relief to get to the end, I realise, but on the other hand, there was also a direct link to what we were singing and the way I began to feel. All things can indeed be bright and beautiful. They usually are. But it hit me at that moment that they were far from bright and beautiful for April.'

There was a real sense of togetherness that morning. People still showed a strong desire to bring April home. It was an occasion when 'tight-knit' was no cliché.

On leaving the church, the Bishop stopped to speak to those who had been standing outside. He emphasised the need to live each minute as it came and that people needed an outlet – such as the one they had just shared together – in order to support each other.

Once outside, Kathleen Rogers began to appreciate the size of the crowd that had assembled around the church. Until then she had no idea what was going on outside. And it wasn't until she got home and saw the television coverage of the morning's events that she got the full picture of the way the town had pulled together. It was obvious that the healing process was beginning, even though the grief was only beginning to take hold.

On Sunday 23 September 2001, New York's Yankee Stadium was the scene of a mass gathering called Prayer for America. It was organised by the city's mayor in order to bring people together after 9/11. One man who took part that day was David Benke, president of the Atlantic District of the Lutheran Church and president of the Lutheran Disaster Response of New York. He said of that event, that the 'process of healing had to begin in the midst of the grief, in order for New Yorkers to believe that healing was even possible'. He then, later, urged people throughout the world, who faced tragedy in their communities, to respond in the same way.

'My strong encouragement and advice is for civic and

religious leaders not to delay in bringing citizens together at a time of crisis, so that the hope of healing can begin.'

The service at St Peter's on Sunday reflected the hope that healing was beginning in Machynlleth. In that particular community, it wasn't organised by civic leaders; a service that would have happened anyway was turned into a community service searching for meaning and healing, offering comfort and solidarity to a fractured community. That's how things are done in Machynlleth.

Kathleen Rogers, nor hardly anyone else, realised that in that procession down from the Bryn y Gog estate to the centre of town were April's parents. As the crowds gathered on the estate and the procession began before the service started, mayor Gareth Jones was approached and asked if he was leading it. He wasn't there in any official capacity and didn't have his chain of office. He said that he was happy to do so and consulted his fellow councillor, Michael Williams, who lives on Bryn y Gog. They agreed that they both would lead from the front. The media attention was firmly focused on the two councillors walking at the head of the procession. Unknown to most, Coral and Paul had taken their place in the middle of the procession too, surrounded by a throng of plain-clothes police. They marched in dignified silence with everyone else, unnoticed by the world's media. When the procession arrived at the town centre, and turned right at the clock towards the church, Coral and Paul turned with them and walked for the next few hundred yards. Then, as the procession turned left off the main road towards the church gates, Coral and Paul were whisked away to the right up a narrow lane by the side of the Skinners pub. A police car awaited them at the top of the lane to take them home again. But they had stood, side by side with their own, throughout that procession. They identified with the people who had been there for them, tied together by the ribbon of community.

The day of the service marked a milestone in the dramatic April Jones story. There were signs that things were moving on in a different direction again as far as the searching and investigation was concerned. The police announced that the mountain rescue element of the search was being scaled down but that the police efforts were being doubled from that day forwards and concentrating more on the town centre and its immediate surroundings.

In the grounds of the church, on the BBC News channel, a mother and daughter shared what they had done in the town the day before, in the name of the April campaign. They had stood in the town's Co-op all day and collected more than £1,000 for the fund. That work would carry on with a vengeance as that first week became the second.

The search for April had an unexpected effect on two of the town's sporting traditions in those early days too. The search coincided with the beginning of the snooker league season. The vast majority of the men who would have been involved in that league were out looking for April. As a result, there was soon to be a backlog of unplayed games for the town team. They were unable to play a meaningful part in the league and had to then effectively cancel their entire season.

The town, as stated previously, is a football town when it comes to ball games. The town's team plays on a pitch near the Leisure Centre and Y Plas. From the early days of the inquiry, that pitch was needed by the police and TV crews for their helicopters. The football club contacted officials of their Aberystwyth League and asked for permission to cancel their forthcoming games. The request was made in the early days of the investigation and the response noted the rule of needing to give three weeks' warning before cancelling. But once league officials were made fully aware of the situation, the Machynlleth club had full backing to suspend their games. This had a considerable knock-on effect on the rest of the league, but the cooperation and goodwill was unquestionable.

From the first week, town mayor Gareth Jones began

keeping a record of significant milestones in the way the town reacted to the unfolding story. Some of these were for the press, for publications as diverse as the *Liverpool Daily Post* and the *Big Issue*, while others were related to his official capacity as mayor. They serve as a valuable record of how one of the town's leaders responded to events.

'I remember sitting down to write that first response, two weeks after April was taken. The second sentence of the piece I wrote then says: "... thirteen days later, we are still uncertain about what occurred or what the eventual outcome might be..." Once the news was announced that April was abducted, I noted that the change in the mood in the town was "immediately tangible". What I wrote went on like this:

Children who had previously walked to school alone in assured safety were now transported there by their parents, the normally bustling Maengwyn Street was uncommonly quiet and there was only one topic of conversation in the cafés and pubs. The shock was accompanied by uncertainty, with only very scant information available in the early stages. But this was soon to change, as more news emerged the town was transformed into a world which none of us could recognise, scenes only previously viewed on TV screens were now occurring outside our own front doors and everything took on an unreal, nightmarish feel.

The media was everywhere and the town's normal quietness was shattered. We all just wanted to wake up and find out it had all been a bad dream. From that day onwards the Dyfi Valley lost its innocence forever.

And, as more harrowing news was announced in the coming days, people's lives were turned upside down, their days blurred into one and many did not see their homes for the remainder of the week. Everyone was focused on one thing only – getting April home safely to her devastated family. And there remained an indestructible positiveness, optimism and above all – HOPE.

Much has been reported about the strong community spirit in Machynlleth and how people turned out in their thousands to help in the search for April, this may be foreign to those unaccustomed to life in the Dyfi Valley but it is no surprise to any of us who are from here. We live in an area where people know one another and although we have our differences we will always lookout for and support one another at times of adversity. The procession to the church on Sunday spoke volumes, it brought people of all ages and backgrounds together to walk shoulder to shoulder to St Peter's in support of April and her family and the HOPE that she will be brought home safely.

Now as the search for April enters a different phase the community is working hand in hand with the police to achieve the outcome we are all HOPING for. There are small signs that the town is very gradually trying to return to some sort of normality but it is undeniable that this will take many months or years before we will come to terms with what happened. In the last two dreadful weeks Dyfi Valley people have been in the world's spotlight and have demonstrated what the phrase 'community spirit' really means, we have found an inner strength and will continue to act with our customary calm and dignity – providing continued support to April and her family and showing the world that Machynlleth is still the best and safest place to live and that our HOPE for April remains undiminished.

That's how things were in the town, as seen by its civic leader two weeks after the abduction. Hope was a buzz word, a spirit to cling on to in those weeks despite the fact that a man from the town had been charged with both the abduction and murder of April Jones. Another two weeks later, a month since April had gone missing, Gareth Jones was to write the following words:

Today the word HOPE and April's favourite colour pink are what continue to bind our community together. Yes, of course, Machynlleth people are attempting to get their lives back to some type of normality, we have had to return to our day jobs following the awful upheaval of the first week or two, but that does not mean that April and her family are ever far from our thoughts. No matter where you go – whether you are queuing at the post office, shopping in the Co-op, playing in a football match, having a pint in a pub, or if you were part of Saturday's excellent Eisteddfod Powys, you will have heard that word HOPE and seen that colour pink everywhere.

It re-emphasises that the commitment of people of all ages and backgrounds from the Dyfi Valley remains undiminished and as steadfast as we were on October 1st. We still want April home to her family, and our focus will not be diverted from that simple fact until she is found.

Has Machynlleth changed in the last four weeks? Yes, of course it has, that is undeniable.

Five weeks ago this was a town accustomed to being left alone and getting on with its own business. Not any more. That all changed when the seriousness of the situation became apparent when the media arrived and literally put Machynlleth directly under the world's spotlight. Suddenly people who would normally have gone about their duties in assured anonymity were now being thrust in front of TV cameras. In the main this was necessary in order to get the word out there that April was missing, and indeed all those journalists must be commended for their sensitive and excellent reporting, but some people understandably found it intrusive and were glad to see that aspect go.

The police are still here in force and I can say without fear of contradiction that everybody in Machynlleth and the Dyfi Valley has gained a renewed respect for them. Even individuals who may have previously fallen foul of the law have approached me in confidence and said that their opinion of the police has altered immeasurably because of the way that information has been relayed to the public and particularly how our young people are being counselled and cared for. It is also apparent that Dyfed Powys Police have taken the time to understand how Machynlleth people tick – that is very much appreciated and has gained them much respect.

A month on, I know that Machynlleth people are as committed as ever we were to getting April home. Many are diverting their efforts to raising money for April's Fund; it will soon become a registered charity with independent trustees appointed. People are clinging on to the HOPE that April will be brought home safe, but let there be no mistake – living in HOPE is essential and should not be confused with living in denial; we are hard-headed realists in the Dyfi Valley and are starkly aware of the difference.

The togetherness of the people of the Dyfi Valley has been commented upon many times over the previous four weeks and I know that we all feel very proud of how our community has bound together and gained additional strength from one another. I know too that we, as a town, will recover from this; we have always put our young people first and we owe it to them to show the way forward, acting with our renowned calm and dignity. Machynlleth is and always will be a safe and beautiful place to live.

The hope and sense of community pride is more than evident in these words. There's an innocence here that refuses to be tarnished, it refuses to be down-trodden by the evil that has evidently befallen them as a society. It is not a saccharine innocence though, one that's blind to the existence of evil in a pie-in-the-sky way. It realises what is, more than likely, to be the harsh, evil truth, but refuses to let that realisation be affected by any negative attitude.

This strong community attitude was recognised by many outsiders, among them the Co-operative Society. In 2012 they decided unequivocally that their prized award, the Robert Owen Award for Outstanding Contribution to Cooperation, should be awarded to the people of Machynlleth. Robert Owen was a pioneering industrialist who was born not far from Machynlleth, in Newtown. He was a social reformer who experimented with various forms of social and industrial communities in London, the USA and Scotland. He is widely regarded as the father of the Co-operative movement. The following citation was read out at the award ceremony by June Jones, chair of the Co-operative Group, Mid Wales:

These awards were created to recognise and celebrate exceptional examples of cooperation in Wales. Today's recipients, thus far, have been individuals and members of an organization, but this final award goes to the people of a whole town.

The overwhelming sense of community and cooperation in the face of the tragic disappearance of one of its own, little April Jones, has attracted the attention of the world.

The people of Machynlleth have shown us, in a truly moving way, that we do not live isolated lives. We are all members of a wider community that come together in good times and bad.

The people of Machynlleth made us all wish that we lived in

such a caring and cooperative community. You have shown the finer aspects of the human wish to work together.

On behalf of the Co-operative Group, it is a real privilege to ask the mayor of Machynlleth, Councillor Gareth Jones, and the mayoress of Machynlleth, Eirwen Edwards, to collect this Robert Owen Award 2012 for outstanding contribution to cooperation on behalf of the people of Machynlleth.

Gareth Jones's response was very similar to the words he had made public a few weeks earlier. He added these words:

> This award is for every person in Machynlleth without exception. For the hundreds of volunteers who searched tirelessly for days on end, for the people who contributed and made food for the emergency services, for the young children of our town whose lives became traumatised at the scenes unfolding before them, for the elderly and disabled people who suffered sleepless nights at the thought of how their beloved home town was being devastated, for the members of the farming community who turned out in such great numbers to assist in the searches, for the teachers and teaching assistants whose care of our young people is exemplary, the list goes on and our efforts will continue unabated.
>
> Our thoughts remain very much with April Jones and her family at this time and we continue to live in hope.

Meanwhile, Christmas was drawing nearer. In the aftermath of 1 October, the usual Christmas celebrations were going to be difficult in Machynlleth. On the one hand, everything seemed to be going on positively, with no let-up in the activity in the name of April, as the fundraising continued relentlessly. The week before the town was awarded their Robert Owen Prize, an auction had raised more than £4,000 for the fund, thanks, in part, to donations by Catherine Zeta Jones and Bonnie Tyler. The response was worldwide. This meant that the fund by the first week of December had raised more than £50,000.

But side-by-side with this, the town's leaders knew that they had to prepare the usual celebrations for Christmas, while still honouring the memory of a child from the town who would not be able to be part of the celebrations. Each group who had a connection to the tragedy had to deal with it in their own way, but everyone was adamant that the children of the town had to be given a Christmas they would be proud of too.

'The school needed to deal with the approach to Christmas in their own way,' says the mother of a six-year-old boy, 'and that was absolutely right. As a parent, I'm sure I can speak for so many others when I say that it was a massive time of conflicting feelings that were pulling against each other. We felt so guilty that we were thinking of preparing for Christmas as usual, knowing that Paul and Coral had no chance to do anything like we were thinking of doing. The guilt was terrible. Then as soon as those kinds of feelings started to take over, we felt even more guilty that we had felt guilty about giving our own children a 'normal' Christmas – that we'd actually thought we needed to deny our own children. There was no way of winning.'

In the end, the whole town pulled together to try and make Christmas 2012 as normal as possible for the children of Machynlleth. While Halloween and Bonfire Night had both been observed since April was taken, they were not marked as they had been in previous years in Machynlleth. At Christmas time the lights went up in the town, and this year they included a metre-tall pink star that was there to remember April. All other lights were switched off every night – but April's star wasn't.

Turning on the Christmas tree and lights was organised as usual, with many other events planned for the day too. The day began with a Christmas market at Y Plas, with local produce on sale. The pensioners' Christmas tea was held at 3 p.m., with the Girl Guides, Brownies and Rainbows performing Christmas carols at both events. A children's disco and party followed at 6 p.m. at Y Plas, with the usual visit from Father Christmas.

Everyone then left Y Plas to form a procession to walk the few hundred yards up to the town clock, where the Christmas tree lights would be switched on officially. Normally it was the town mayor's privilege to switch those lights on, but on this occasion Gareth Jones chose to forgo that duty.

'This year I wanted the emphasis to be on the children of our town, and my idea of asking them all to count down the seconds until the lights came on, as if by magic, was a conscious effort to make them all feel equally important after what they had endured over the previous two months. What I did was hide myself out of sight and flicked the switch at the relevant time as the town clock chimed 6.30 p.m., so the kids thought they had turned the Christmas lights on – it worked a treat and the whole day was a great success.'

The attendance at the 2012 turning-on of the Christmas tree lights was far better than many previous years. There were hundreds there and police regulated the traffic through the town. There was a Nativity scene underneath the clock for the first time, and the community carol singing was far more robust than usual.

'Christmas was an awful time, a difficult time to say the least,' says Kathleen Rogers. 'Everybody tried really, really hard to make things all right for the children. They needed that.'

'There were a lot of frightened children in the town,' says David Williams, a father in his 40s. 'There were a lot of frightened adults here too. We were confused and Christmas gave us a focus.'

A great deal of effort had gone into that one day leading up to Christmas. As they had stood and sat together in that church service the Sunday after April went missing, so they stood together again at Christmas. But, by that time, the questions had changed.

'Every conversation on the street when you were out shopping,' says Kathleen Rogers, 'began in a normal conversational way as we consciously tried to chat about day-to-day things. But every conversation almost always ended up discussing April's story. We were confused, there's no doubt. We wanted to know why, why did it happen to us, exactly what had happened. There was no shortage of questions and we would talk to each other about those questions in order to try and get some answers. We didn't have any big answers mind, but those chats were very much needed.'

The landlord of one of the town's pubs summed it up by saying that April's name was mentioned within ten minutes of any conversation starting in his pub. People of all ages, all backgrounds, would be part of this community questioning, the communal search for answers.

Mayor Gareth Jones's Christmas letter ended on a very different note in 2012. Having mentioned the notable success achieved by many from the town during the previous twelve months, he turned to the one big, dark, shadow over their year, and concludes:

> It is difficult to predict how events will unfold in the year ahead, just as nobody could have envisaged how 2012 would have turned out. The search for April Jones continues; she and her family are very much at the forefront of our minds and we live in hope. As we prepare to face the uncertainties of 2013 together, if I were to sum up my feelings towards my home town in one word, that word would be 'pride'. Everybody in Machynlleth can take great pride in the dignity and strength we have shown over the last year and I personally am proud to have been their mayor during this time, but more than that I am proud to say that I am from Machynlleth and that I am surrounded by the most determined, caring, considerate, talented and dignified people in the world.

As 2012 drew to a close, the spirit of Christmas mingled with the spirit of Hope that the town of Machynlleth had shown for nearly three months. They were trying to keep an impossible normality. What helped them to begin to achieve this was an unquestionable sense of identity, a robust sense of pride in who they were as a people.

5

Healing words and hugs

April's story is an extremely personal, family tragedy. But from the first few hours of her disappearance, it was also, in a very real way, the living experience of a Welsh community. As events unfolded, it was to become the experience of a far wider, international community.

Other communities throughout Britain and further afield have experienced similar tragedies over the years, of course. But there was something different, something more than noteworthy about the way the Dyfi Valley community responded and reacted to April's disappearance. Not necessarily better than the way other places had responded to tragic events, as better is a meaningless concept in such circumstances. But certainly different.

From the moment April Jones was taken, Machynlleth would never be the same again – its people don't want it to be. They're not fooled by any suggestion that they should try to carry on as normal, because they know that things aren't normal. They're not lulled into a false sense of security that the whole idea of what's called 'closure' actually exists, let alone worry whether it is imminent or not.

By the time that October day was drawing to a close and word had got round Machynlleth that little April was missing, no sooner had people heard than they were out looking for her in the many ways we've already read about. For eight months, from that first day of October until the end of Mark Bridger's trial, they had to deal with unprecedented internal anguish and turmoil, while at the same time dealing with being utterly exposed to the gaze of the world's media. Questions came and went with both a randomness and an intensity that was always overwhelming. Searching for answers was the second extensive exercise they'd have to do since 1 October. And, as with the physical search for April, this personal quest took the people of Machynlleth to uncharted territory, rough terrain and isolated places. It would leave a people weary and emotional, but the same determination that saw them persevere in their searching would see them through the difficult questions. Except that this quest is likely to last a lot longer, and with no more likelihood of there being a definite ending than there was of finding April.

They were, naturally enough, questions to do with the search for meaning and understanding, early and confused attempts at making sense of the moral chaos they had been thrown into. The pavement conversations, the discussions over a pint or a coffee, all in the name of finding the 'sense' that Kathleen Rogers said they were trying to grasp at. How did the mind and actions of an evil man play in the bigger picture of a traditional community's daily life? How did the taking of one of their children affect those left behind? The criminal proceedings might well be over now, and Mark Bridger has started to live the rest of his life in jail, but there's no doubt that the town itself is still struggling, indeed agonising, to try and find answers to so many disturbing questions, because they have to live with the whole story in a way that no other community has to. It's their attempts to fathom, to reconcile the disparate voices whirling around inside their heads and their souls that we hear on these pages. Mixed in with those central voices are those that are heard from the wings, maybe not at centre stage, but no less significant or heartfelt, as they share their reaction to the story from their perspective, from their diverse motives and associations, from their different countries. Many voices have reached Machynlleth. Mass public grief has been very prominent, whether the grievers knew April Jones or not.

Nowhere felt all these whirlwinds of emotions and the full force of the deep-seated grief more than the school where April was a pupil. That's where she was on that last Monday. That's where her friends went back to after everyone knew she had disappeared. That's where the empty chair was.

The school has had to deal with what could be described as a more concentrated form of grief because there's a perimeter fence to hold it in and there are brick walls inside that fence. Within those walls, it's hard to imagine what the head teacher and her staff had to deal with. Each child would have had his or her own way of reacting to what had happened, or what they thought had happened, to the little girl in the classroom down the corridor, to their friend April.

There have been many conversations with Gwenfair Glyn, the head teacher of Machynlleth Primary School, in preparing this book. Those discussions about how the school and its teachers and pupils coped with the tragedy have been both difficult and painfully honest. There was no lack of a desire to cooperate, but the feeling of sheer numbness about the whole situation and the complex nature of the school's reactions to it meant that sharing it at any length in this book was not possible at this time. With this frame of mind being so obvious and so deep, it was agreed that there would be no long discussions about how the school has been affected and no detailed accounts of how the school actually did deal with the trauma in the months from October until the end of the school year in July 2013.

During those telephone conversations with the head teacher, some points mentioned by her are included where relevant in these pages, with her consent. But, generally, it was decided to leave the impact of the tragic event on the school outside the remit of this book. No teacher could imagine what it could have been like for their colleagues at Machynlleth Primary School, to have one of their own taken in such circumstances. No teaching course can prepare any one in charge of a classroom or a school for such a tragedy.

October: The crowds gather at Machynlleth Leisure Centre.

Sky News interview mayor Gareth Jones.

Police from many areas search the Dyfi Valley.

© Iestyn Hughes

The longest police search in British criminal history gathers momentum – in the fields and in the control room.

People gather as one, quietly and in hope, to offer their services and hear the latest news.

With her missing daughter looking over her shoulder, a distraught Coral faces the world's media.

The intensive land and river search continues.

Searching in the shadow of irony.

Ceinws, where pleas for help stand near Mark Bridger's white cottage.

© Daily Post

Y Plas, Machynlleth, centre of operations.

© Daily Post

Rescue and emergency teams search the dense woodlands.

Friends and neighbours gather in procession on the Bryn y Gog estate.

The procession soon fills the streets of Machynlleth town centre.

© Iestyn Hughes

Young and old sit and wait in the churchyard as the service continues inside.

Reverend Kathleen Rogers and the Right Reverend Andrew John, Bishop of Bangor, lead the community in expectation and healing.

© Daily Post

The candle of hope is lit.

GWEDDIWN DROS
APRIL JONES
A'I THEULU.

DAD NEFOL
N DY DRUGAREDD
ANDO EIN GWEDDIAU.

WE PRAY FOR
APRIL JONES
AND
HER FAMILY.

HEAVENLY FATHER
YOUR TENDER MERCY
HEAR OUR PRAYERS.

A town unites in quiet respect.

2012/10/01 17:29:57

The last image of April, hours before she was taken.

The garden at Bryn y Gog, with April's home in the background.

The Hugging Tree, simple, spiritual.

The pink ribboned promenade at Aberystwyth, a silent tribute near the sea.

April's memory is prominent in all community events. Messages and memorials far and wide:

… a neon tribute on the roadside

… from the troops in Afghanistan

… a statue in Barmouth, north Wales

… a shrine in Tenby, south Wales

Three buildings lit in pink tribute: Blackpool Tower, Carmarthen County Hall and Machynlleth Clock Tower.

Top Gear remembers

Ribbons… ready to leave Wheeler's in Machynlleth

… as does Eddie Stobart lorries

… and the sporting world

… on the gate of April's school

… on the doors of houses

… on The Jacobite, the steam train between Fort William and Mallaig

Wales football manager Chris Coleman with Paul, Coral, Harley and Jasmine at a fundraising football match in Machynlleth.

A permanent reminder of the need for hope.

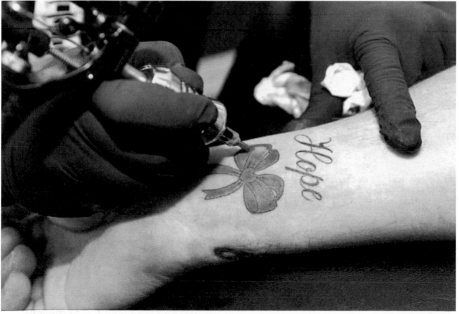

Hope – painted in faint pink on a rock overlooking the town of Machynlleth.

And, of course, the teachers themselves had to deal with their own grief in their own way, while holding the hands of the young ones in their care.

The reaction of others in schools across the world where similar tragedies have happened has been well documented. From such research we can begin to understand what might have been going on in the Machynlleth Primary School for nearly a whole school year. The National Institute of Mental Health, in a study published after the Twin Tower bombings in New York on 9/11, says that the more direct exposure children have to the traumatic event, the greater the likelihood of psychological stress and harm. This does not necessarily mean actually witnessing the event. Proximity is the issue – having a close link to the person or persons who have died. Proximity is also influenced by the child's perception of the level of threat to his or her life after the tragedy and the level of disruption to their lives after the event, particularly at home and in school. There was a close proximity between what happened to April Jones and the children in the same school as her.

But the same study also emphasises that the reaction of significant adults is an important influence on the way children deal with any psychological stress and harm. Children will take their cues from adults, such as parents and teachers. This is particularly true when that reaction of adults is formalised and structured in a care programme to deal with the children's feelings. If the situation isn't dealt with, if the child perceives an element of disorder or disruption on behalf of the adults, within the school setting in this case, then the adverse psychological effects on the children are likely to increase. From the first moment that Machynlleth Primary School realised what was happening, their reaction was controlled and structured. The children's response was managed. Many parents have testified to that.

Children's questions needed to be dealt with. Children's out-of-character silences needed to be addressed. There were as many ways of reacting to the news that April had gone as there were children in the school. And, as children are in school for such a long time, a great deal of their reaction and attempts at understanding what had happened occurred during school hours. If dealt with during that time, the managing of emotions has the added benefit that those children then return home having been properly assessed. That then has the additional effect of transferring positive impetus to the wider community.

'Schools are in a unique position to prepare and help community members,' as bereavement counsellor Barbara L Bouton says, 'to understand and respond to tragic experiences that affect children's lives.' Without doubt Machynlleth Primary School played a central role during that first week in managing the crisis and helping the whole community begin to deal with the situation. It's too soon to say what the real effect will be on its pupils – that will unfold over time. But the critical, initial response was certainly on the right footing and set the foundation for the various ways of responding that would inevitably follow.

Early in the investigation, within two days of the news of April's disappearance, a table was placed in the foyer of the school as a way of showing both support and hope. April's fellow pupils made ribbons to be placed on the table and a book was laid open on it so that children, staff and parents could write any message they wished to the school or Paul and Coral. It was a constant reminder of the hope that was apparent throughout the community.

Children were given leaflets to take home, noting that help was available if it was needed. Some did take up the offer. And the teachers have been praised for the sheer hard work they put into deal with the questioning and the need to talk by many parents. Many families, however, didn't know how to respond to such an offer of help.

'We knew, I suppose, that we needed help,' one of the mothers on Bryn y Gog estate says, 'but we had no idea what kind, or help for what specifically. You could say that we were still taking it all in, not knowing what was really going on. But it was good to know that help was there if we needed it.'

Children and teachers alike, along with the rest of the town, fell into an instinctive way of responding to an event both traumatic and challenging to our perceptions and comforts. They started to think 'what if?'. They wondered how things would have turned out if one of the minor events leading up to the tragedy hadn't happened. That changes nothing, of course, but we feel the need to include such an exercise in processing what happened. These are questions which Paul and Coral have both intimated to a degree in interviews – how, if their actions had been different on that Monday, things might have happened differently for their daughter.

The same sort of questioning tormented the families of James Bulger, Jessica Chapman and Holly Wells. Two-year-old James Bulger disappeared while out shopping with his mum on 12 February 1993. His body was discovered on a nearby railway track two days later. Jessica and Holly disappeared on 4 August 2002, having been playing at Holly's home after a barbecue. The bodies of the two ten-year-old girls were found two weeks later. In all cases, their parents were in close proximity.

How Paul and Coral will articulate their feelings will be revealed over time, one suspects. They certainly weren't in any position to put any sense of order to their thoughts and emotions for this publication. But the same type of questioning, the 'what if?', *has* been on the lips of the people of Machynlleth.

What if April hadn't had a swimming lesson that day to perk her up after school? She might well have gone home tired, had tea, watched a film and stayed in and gone to bed. What if Mark Bridger hadn't been dumped that day and he had gone in to work as normal? There are so many permutations, but not one of them excuses or justifies Mark Bridger's actions and no-one else can be blamed for doing something that should have been done differently, with different consequences. They're all questions trying to make sense of the irrational, unexplainable evil. These are some of the questions at least. The 'what if?' and 'why?' are always harder if the reason behind the questioning is suddenly thrust upon those asking.

And it was thrust upon Machynlleth of course, happening so quickly on that first day of October, those few horrendous minutes when a family, a man and a community shared the same event in chillingly different ways. What actually happened to April remains locked in the sick mind of one man, although what emerged during the court case is more than anyone need begin to contemplate. From that first day, there's been a whirlwind of emotion tearing through people's lives: anger, anguish, resolve, love, hate, support, solidarity and dignity. In so many ways, April Jones's story has touched, shaken, affected and challenged individuals, communities and institutions alike. And it has brought strangers together.

Local parents, of course, still have to deal with their children's reaction. One very visible cause of concern, and quite often a very real fear, is explained by the mother of a ten-year-old girl.

'What really frightened my daughter and made her feel quite agitated were the helicopters that circled in the air above our town. There was an obvious difference why the police helicopters were there and why the camera helicopters were there, but when you're a frightened child, a helicopter looming out of nowhere is extremely disturbing. Other parents have told me that they would have been walking with their children in the hills and a helicopter would come over the top of a hill without warning right in front of us. It was very, very scary.'

Another mum adds, 'As adults, we might well be able to see that there's a difference between a police helicopter there to do its job in helping to find April and a camera crew helicopter there to find whatever it can find. But that doesn't mean for us that we are any less scared for knowing. Imagine how it feels for a child. The thrill of seeing a helicopter up close soon goes when it happens unexpectedly time and time again in the place you live.'

Another parent added that this was a particular concern in one specific place: 'The constant presence of the TV crew helicopters specifically hovering above the school, time after time, did make things really difficult for both staff and pupils at the school. It was a very intrusive presence, a horrible, aggressive reminder of what had happened. Whatever was being done inside the school to deal with children's reactions to April's story, could be undone in a second if a camera helicopter flew overhead looking for that one cheap shot.'

How would parents and teachers deal with such an issue? What would they say? The helicopters were seen as an aggressive violation, literally shattering any peace they might have managed to piece together in the community. But locals also knew that they were needed – a necessary evil. Parents talk of having the situation at home relatively under control, but then outside factors, such as helicopters and a knock on the door from the police, would disrupt the way they were dealing with issues within their four walls. Parents' own reactions were difficult enough to deal with, regardless of any outside interruption, especially for those who lived on Bryn y Gog estate. One mother sums up what was said by many:

'The real difficulty was knowing whether to say anything or not. Sometimes, if you could see they were upset then obviously a reassuring *cwtsh* was needed, a few words of comfort and maybe a longer chat. But there were so many times that you really didn't know whether to ask if they were OK or not. Maybe, at that particular point, they were actually OK and just the fact of me bringing the question up would bring the whole issue to the surface and make things not OK again.'

'You just don't want to put your child in a situation where they're forced to talk about something they don't want to,' a father in his 40s remarks. 'Initially the questions were mainly factual, asking for different bits of information about the story, trying to piece together the structure of the story, if you like, the actual narrative. Then as that first week went on and certainly after that, the questions were different, more in search of an understanding.'

Some children could process the events in a seemingly

straightforward way, with a childlike simplicity that belies the horror of what happened. Two sets of parents said that their children had turned to them one day and said categorically and without any seeming emotion, that April must by now have been dead because she had probably gone so long without food and water. In both cases, such a reaction gave the parents more to deal with than the child. But parents can't always control the way their children deal with such a tragedy.

'I was at work one day,' a single mother from Bryn y Gog explains, 'when I had a call from my mum saying that my son was upset. On asking a little bit more I gathered that my mum had a conversation with him about April and told him that April was dead. I was fuming! I had to leave work there and then and, as soon as I got home, my boy ran towards me, into my arms and burst out crying. He was uncontrollable. I was not happy that the whole thing had been dealt with in the way it had. He didn't ask for the conversation. But then again, on looking back at it, my mum had emotions to deal with too, I suppose she was genuine enough in not wanting my boy to suffer in silence, so she thought she was helping. I don't suppose that any of us knew the right way to react. You don't exactly get time to prepare for something like this.'

Another dad shared a sense of helplessness with regards to how to deal with his son: 'I know there's stuff there, but I just don't know how much.'

Machynlleth had never experienced a week like that one in October last year. Thrown together by what was at first thought to be no more than misfortune, united in the physical act of searching for a little girl, and then the bond intensifies as the news breaks that a murder inquiry is now in place. That raw spirit of togetherness, fledgling and uncertain, saw the townspeople turn from searchers to supporters, volunteers to fundraisers before, finally, being mourners together, claiming the town's streets and its church for April and affirming a town's sense of hope.

In Machynlleth Primary School, as the end of the school

year approached in July 2013, the whole story, and its effects on staff and pupils, was addressed. It was decided to hold an end-of-term service on the last Thursday before the summer holidays. The aim was to bring the whole story to as dignified, but definite, end as was possible. Photographs of April during her years at the school were gathered together and words written by some of the pupils were read out. April's story was put in the wider context of beginning and end, life and death, so that the children could learn about April's place in the bigger story of life. There was an aim to regard this service as a way of ensuring that issues and situations would not carry over to the beginning of the new school year in September. The school felt that it needed to draw some sort of line under the events before moving on and facing, potentially, a new surge in interest in the autumn, a year since her disappearance.

For many, the service was welcomed. But it wasn't a unanimous feeling. Three mums said that their children had been upset seeing all the photographs of April gathered together on that day. They didn't like going over the story once more. It was an indication that people were beginning to respond differently. That end-of-school-year service proved to be a tough time for one child in particular, the daughter of Mark Bridger. She had previously gone through the annual school sports day with no difficulties, being a member of the same school 'house' as April's brother. But, the service was more difficult to deal with, and she was overcome by the occasion. Whether that was because of missing April or because she realised the significance of who her father was, we shall never know. It's another example of just what the school has had to deal with during those harrowing months: the brother of the victim and the daughter of the murderer in the same school house.

One other story from the school, on first hearing, may well have a more sinister tone to it. One or two parents and one of the rescue team leaders too, say they became aware of children adapting a school playground game and calling it the Mark Bridger and April Jones game. It's not as macabre as it may sound and is indeed not an uncommon local response to such tragedies. There are other instances of children in schools near similar tragedies adapting their play to reflect those stories. In south Wales, following a search for a woman with mental health issues who'd gone missing in the Brecon Beacons, children in a nearby school were seen to play a game they called 'Find Julie' (the woman's name has been changed). At the end of the day, what such childlike playground activity does is reflect what the community they are part of feels is real at that time. The children pick up the dominant community feeling and give it their own innocent treatment.

Other schools throughout Wales and beyond had to react and respond to April's story. Eighty miles south of Machynlleth, the children of Ysgol Gymraeg Parc y Tywyn, in Burry Port, are representative of what other schools had to deal with. One of their teachers, Adam Barnett, who teaches eight- and nine-year-olds, clearly remembers arriving at school on 2 October.

'When I walked into my class, as normal, I soon realised that the children were all talking about what had happened in Machynlleth the day before. They had no concept at all of where Machynlleth was, but they knew it was in Wales. It was obviously a real issue for them all and I realised that it needed to be dealt with.'

Adam, a young teacher in his 20s, admits that he had no specific knowledge of how to deal with such a situation. Teachers' training is about subjects and teaching methods, not how to tell children about the murder of another child. But he knew he had to deal with the situation he was confronted with.

'The children were saying what mum or dad had said about the story, they wanted to know what I thought had happened. Surprisingly, many said it was like Madeleine McCann's story, even though I didn't think they were old enough to remember that. They must have been told that by their parents. I had to carefully explain that evil or bad things happen sometimes, but we were to put it in a broader context of good and evil.

'It was an eye-opener for me in that it made me realise that children see the same news, receive the same information as we adults do. They take the same things in and they need to be helped to deal with it. And, of course, it made me think that if our children were going through what they were going through, what on the earth were the children in April's school facing? It was impossible to think about that.'

It's far too soon to know exactly what the children of Machynlleth have been through. It's too soon to know how they have been affected. Initially, on the Bryn y Gog estate specifically, there would be no children out playing on the grassy areas in between the rows of houses or among the garages. Over time, children have returned to play there now, parents and children alike regaining confidence in the outdoors, security in their surroundings. But what goes on inside the minds of the children and parents will only gradually unravel over time.

6

A place to talk

MACHYNLLETH COULD NOT be described as a place where counselling and therapy techniques would readily be accepted as part of its culture. Traditionally, it would be similar to the agriculture- and religion-dominated Northern Ireland. During that country's troubles, its first police ombudsman, Nuala O'Loan, commented on the way that the majority of communities affected by the killings and bombings had dealt with their tragedies:

'The traditional Irish way of dealing with grief is not to talk. There have been families here, when someone has been killed and the decision has been taken – "We will never speak of this". That closes people down and then maybe 20 or 30 years later the trauma manifests itself in ways that people don't understand.'

Machynlleth 2012 was a more complex, diverse community than the Irish one described by O'Loan. There was indeed that curtain of silence, but there were also those who felt the need to search for help in their own personal quests for answers to those questions.

And in the town, an early way of responding to the constant questioning and the clouds of grief was a counselling service which was set up by volunteers under the direction of a qualified therapist. Dr Susan Dale, who lives in Machynlleth, has been working professionally as a counsellor for the past 15 years and is an accredited member of the BACP (British Association of Counselling and Psychotherapy). As April's story was unfolding, she was more than aware of the growing need among her fellow Machynlleth people for what could be described as therapeutic support. While the search was still in its early days, she went to speak to those among the Dyfed Powys Police team who were responsible for welfare issues and voiced her opinion that help was needed. Susan Dale, a trustee of Wales-wide counselling charity, CCSW, also talked with her fellow trustees, asking if their work could be channelled to help in Machynlleth.

Some other agencies also prepared a counselling service of sort, and some counsellors were sent to Machynlleth. But the service in a town centre building was not well used. It was still early days, with the same uncertainty in the air as was on that first Monday night at Bryn y Gog, when the enthusiastic volunteers knew why they were there but didn't know exactly what to do. Dealing with the subsequent reaction, feelings and grief, was directionless for a while. This same initial expression of help was shown after 9/11 in New York. In writing about that tragedy later, David A Thomson, who runs an independent counselling service in Minnesota, and Edward J Holland, the coordinator of grief support at a hospice in Minneapolis, describe the tendency to depend too much on the first response:

'One of the difficulties in helping those affected by public tragedies in making sense and meaning out of sudden human-caused losses is that we are not well prepared to provide long-term interventions in people's lives. Instead we tend to be geared to respond with quick fixes promoting the illusion that life can get back to normal quickly.'

They then add that there is a need for this first response from medical and healthcare professionals, but that when they leave the scene of tragedy, further issues are raised: '... after the initial interventions survivors are often left to ponder the deeper questions on their own, with limited long-term support for this task. Culturally and institutionally, we are not prepared to engage in serious long-term discussions and interventions after disasters.'

The attempts in Machynlleth to provide a first response to

the taking of April Jones has led to a far longer term approach. The Listening Point service set up by Susan Dale is still available a year later.

'There was a feeling in October of, "so what exactly do we need?" in Machynlleth at such a time. The answer was that we probably needed lots of different approaches because the situation was evidently so severe. But the obvious need for me was for a centre, a room, whatever form it took, where people could call in, for a tea or a coffee and a chat if they so wished. They could only chat about the weather if that's what they wanted, but at least there was talking and people were less isolated.'

This need became more pronounced as the first few days turned into weeks. When those from the local and wider community were out searching together, they were talking to each other. But as the search came to an end, opportunities to converse lessened. The voluntary organising of supplies and fundraising was more fragmented and haphazard than the structured team searching.

'It could be said, in a careful and considered way, that the mood was better when the volunteers were out en masse together. Once the police took over, as they rightly had to do, the mood changed. People were quieter. The situation became more fragmented as people didn't have anyone to share with so readily and they were almost stuck with the feelings and questions they had.'

Susan Dale's observations ring true with many townspeople spoken to. It reflects an attitude of being faced with having to ask, for the first time ever, 'what actually is normal behaviour?' As one writer put it, 'A tragedy makes us ask questions we've never asked before.'

'Was it right to smile now? Should I laugh or is it wrong to do that?' asks one father from an outlying village.

A mother from Bryn y Gog shares her difficulty in addressing the same issue: 'It was really hard to know how to carry on with our day-to-day life. I know I would go about my day in such-and-such a way, with thoughts of what happened to April raw in my mind, and I would ask myself is this the right way to be, or is this just the way of the town now, because of what's happened? I don't suppose there is one answer.'

Author Mike Parker lived in Ceinws for ten years, the village where Mark Bridger's home was, and where, probably, April's short life came to an end. He's very much aware of how the events of the last year have affected his former neighbours.

'I have no doubt that people in Ceinws have been hit very hard. There's a terrible feeling in the village, one I don't think they expected and I think they're not letting on how they have actually been affected. They were thrown into this story and, slowly, over the months, events have seeped into their consciousness like a poison. On the surface there's a strong sense of getting on with it, but not underneath.'

Mike Parker suggests that the physical disruption to village life and its properties plays a major part in the way Ceinws people now feel.

'In terms of the amount of digging of gardens done by the searchers, the searching of houses, out-houses and any other buildings, Ceinws has had more than anywhere else. There are a lot of questions and troubled souls in what is essentially a small hamlet.'

As well as contacting Dyfed Powys Police, Susan Dale also spoke at length to Kathleen Rogers. 'Kath had been superb from the very first day in the way she had stood alongside the community. That was obviously one very good reason to hear how she saw things. But also, she was a local person. I have lived here for quite a while, but I am aware I am an outsider. I don't speak Welsh and, if I'm honest, I don't always get the culture, I don't always get it right and I needed to check that what I thought was needed would actually resonate with the community.'

Susan Dale also spoke to a friend of hers who was living in Dunblane at the time of the tragedy there, when a former Scout leader, Thomas Hamilton, shot dead 16 children and one teacher in the local school in 1996. Susan Dale's research involved seeking information as to how that community responded to its horrific tragedy. Her work pointed to the need for a drop-in centre as well as a helpline and a referral system that could direct those in need to further professional help. Funding also proved to be forthcoming, both from the Church in Wales and the Presbyterian Church in Wales. In addition, the Iona Community, an ecumenical organisation promoting peace and justice, promised both support and funding for a counselling service. By November, there was sufficient funding in place and a week before Christmas, a drop-in centre was opened in the parish office in Machynlleth town centre.

'We were determined to be open by Christmas because we knew that would be a time when people would feel things to be particularly difficult. We opened on Wednesday and Saturday afternoons at first. Wednesday is when the market is in town, and it's always busy, as is Saturday. We also had the phone lines sorted in order to be able to offer a phone-in facility, whereby people could phone for a chat.'

Volunteers were quickly, but thoroughly, trained to deal with the demand, and the service soon had a team of eight core volunteer listeners, with an additional two volunteer counsellors. These volunteers, of course, were also affected by the tragedy themselves and had to listen to, and help, others who had been equally affected. Many of the volunteers have been with the service from the beginning and are still there, others have joined and they form a strong team.

In the first few months of this facility many people called in. Most of those who did were from the immigrant English community, with only a minority of the indigenous Welsh choosing to walk through the door.

Following the murder of two young girls in Soham, Holly Wells's father, Kevin, confessed that he too was not of the generation who would seek counselling from therapists or go to the GP when depression struck.

'Side-by-side with the drop-in centre, the phone line was

up and running too,' Susan Dale continues. 'The people who contacted us by phone, anxious for help and support, were of a different kind to those who used the drop-in centre. They were more distressed or angry and there were those who just wanted to know what was going on.'

By February, it became apparent that the drop-in centre would need to move from the parish office. Its new location proved to be quite significant. The old Spar shop on the edge of town had been used as an office for European Community Development project, Communities First. It was an ideal building in terms of size. It also happened to be on the Bryn y Gog estate, a stone's throw from April Jones's home.

'We were very reluctant to move from the town centre, to be honest. We were also very conscious that we might actually be too close to Coral and Paul and it might in effect make things more difficult for them. I spoke to the family liaison officer about this potential move to the estate and our concerns as to how it would affect April's parents. He relayed the information to Paul and Coral and they sent the message back to say that they would be pleased if we were there,' says Susan.

'The local authority, the owners of the empty building at Bryn y Gog were inviting tenders for its use and specifically encouraging local charities to show an interest. We declared our interest and our application was successful.'

Once the move was confirmed, Susan Dale and the team of volunteers worked out the best time to make the move – either before the Bridger trial or after it – as moving halfway through would have a destabilising effect on the service provided. It was decided to move before the trial.

'We then, of course, needed to furnish the place we'd acquired, so it was all hands on deck to do so in a very short space of time in the end. My husband went round charity shops looking for dining chairs, someone said they had a rocking chair, someone else brought some tablecloths and so on, until what was an office twelve hours before the opening, was a comfortably and sympathetically-furnished counselling drop-in centre by the time the doors opened. Works of art of various descriptions started to arrive as well, so that the walls and noticeboards were a little more colourful and welcoming.'

Once the counselling service was up and running in its new home, the clientele seemed to change.

'Predominantly now it's the people from Bryn y Gog who call in, not exclusively, but there has been a change. The work has taken on a life of its own since coming here, and one thing that has really caught on in the last few months is that Wednesday afternoons have turned into a knitting afternoon! That was not planned at all. Some of the younger women came here and said that they wanted to learn to knit and then some of the older ladies said that they were willing to teach them. So that's what happened. Recently we have run a couple of creative art sessions, and had great fun with families' screen printing T-shirts.'

It's the women of the estate and the area who tend to use the drop-in centre. But the helpline is the exact opposite, with men most likely to use the phone to ask for help. Some prefer to phone and discuss their issues in their native Welsh language.

'If things are troubling you, you usually want to discuss those things in your native language and that is totally understandable. How families work together, especially very rural families, changes within the Welsh dynamic. I've certainly had a very clear picture over the last few months as to the cultural differences within this one area, and the way that affects how different people deal with the same tragedy. But whatever the language and culture, it's become evident that we need to just be here and people then use this place as they see they need to use it.'

Susan Dale has considerable experience of counselling people in a whole range of differing situations. Confronting this tragedy that hit the town she lives in proved to be a completely new situation for her on a personal level.

'It was a situation that gave me a real dilemma. I just could not get my head around it. Whatever else I've had to face in the past, this situation rendered me completely impotent. You couldn't do anything. You were totally at a loss. But, in a strange way, it has also been what could be described as a privilege, because I have been able to meet some amazing people and to see the positive way that they have dealt with such a nightmare situation, such an outpouring of evil, in a way that has been both humbling and heart-warming.'

Susan Dale has received positive feedback on the services, and continues to do so. One lady comments: 'You begin to think that everyone is coping except you! And then when you start talking you realise they are feeling it too! Sharing things with others seems to help in a strange way, and you start then talking about things, and finding things that are more positive then. It feels really safe here to sit and talk not necessarily about anything in particular, but to share being with others, where no-one judges you. Some people knit, others just sit quiet. Sitting alone is too hard some days.'

As 2012 turned into 2013, the questions continued. The rollercoaster might well have slowed down a little, but the people of Machynlleth were still on that up-and-down journey. When January arrived, they faced Mark Bridger's court case, which was scheduled for the 14th of that month. Mayor Gareth Jones prepared a statement reflecting the thoughts of the people of the area:

> Tomorrow will be a difficult day for us all. It is a day that we knew was going to come and is yet another milestone for our community on what is becoming the ceaseless road to eventually gaining answers to what has occurred and, just as importantly, why it happened. But we must be under no illusions; there may still be a long way to go and we must prepare ourselves for what lies ahead. In terms of the legal process this could be the end of the beginning – not the beginning of the end.
>
> Throughout the horrendous and nightmarish three-and-a-half months Machynlleth and the Dyfi Valley have experienced, our thoughts have remained solely and steadfastly on April, Coral, Paul

and their family. This must not alter; our focus must still be on them, more than ever. We must concentrate on positive things, we must use the word HOPE in every conversation we have and remain strong and dignified for them in everything we do, our community's solidarity has been the benchmark which others elsewhere now aspire to and we must remain every bit an example to the outside world as we were in October.

We will face the next steps together and be there for April's family throughout. And, if necessary, we must be there for one another. Yes, understandably, the attention of the world will be in Mold tomorrow, but our thoughts should be on April, her family and her friends back home here in Machynlleth.

Hope is still written in capital letters in that statement, as it has been from the very first communication. Hope was still felt in capital letters by the people, but the letters were beginning to fade.

During that January court appearance by Bridger, a date was set for the trial at Crown Court, which would be at the end of February. Gareth Jones then released another statement:

The people of Machynlleth and, much more importantly, the family of April Jones, have waited five months for answers to what happened on the 1st of October, 2012. That uncertainty would have torn lesser communities apart, but it has brought us all even closer together than we were before and we have shown the world how strong and determined Dyfi Valley people are.

So now the time has finally arrived for the legal process to take its course and we must allow it to do so unhindered by any hint of speculation or rumour.

Everybody in the Dyfi Valley has been through a life-changing experience during the previous five months, we have united together and stood shoulder to shoulder at every step of this dreadful ordeal. We must now re-double our efforts and be stronger still and keep Coral, Paul and their family paramount in our thoughts.

None of us can predict what lies ahead but we will face it together, we must take care of and comfort those most vulnerable around us and be tolerant of those who may occasionally find it difficult to cope. We will remain calm, strong and dignified, showing the world once again that the Dyfi Valley is the most caring, compassionate and peaceful place to be.

We must prepare ourselves for unpleasant times but together we will be strong.

That trial was then postponed for another two months. The five-month wait turned into seven. As time went on, the situation changed for the people of Machynlleth. During those first few days in October it was a case of constant revelation and reaction as developments unfolded and announcements were made. The questioning at such a time was of a more quick-fire nature, aimless, random, confused and fearful. Then as the months went on, and those revelations and developments were embedded in everyone's minds, the questioning became more considered, with less need to react and more time to reflect.

But the grief and healing hasn't exclusively been channelled and shaped in Christian terms. Maybe it has in public, because of the nature of the town and its surrounding areas. But in other places where tragedy has struck, the prominence of psychics and psychic messages has been apparent too – and Soham is also an example of this.

Kevin and Nicola Wells went to see a medium when their daughter was missing. He told them in detail what he thought had happened to Holly and some days later told them that he had contacted their daughter 'on the other side'. Other mediums also contacted them with information. Kevin Wells wrote everything down that he had been told by all the mediums he'd dealt with, solicited or otherwise. He came to the conclusion, with the benefit of hindsight when the case was closed, that he had some questions to face, especially with regards to the information received from one medium in particular, Dennis Mackenzie.

'I remember telling Nicola that I felt Dennis was a very talented medium. Here now in black and white is startling proof that he is the genuine article. It is a clear first-hand indication that there is something "on the other side". I do not have to debate this with anyone. I've seen it for myself. I am completely unsure as to how this may affect my future thinking on spiritual matters.'

After seeing Dennis Mackenzie and receiving detailed information about his daughter's murder which proved to be startlingly accurate, Kevin Wells also went to church. He talks about going to a service and also going to St Andrew's Church, Soham, on his own one evening.

'I pray, I pray out loud, I cry to God for help. I'll do anything to get my daughter back. My promise of unrealistic future commitments to God in exchange for the chance to see Holly alive and well again, they echo through the dark church.'

Facing the violent taking of the life of a child, your own or someone else's, forces people to ask questions about the whole point of life that would not otherwise have been asked. It's not known if Coral and Paul followed the same path as Kevin and Nicola. But psychics did contact one person very much involved in the Machynlleth story.

'I was contacted many times,' says Alyson Jones from the sweet shop, Losin Lush. 'I had letters sent to me offering information and they were passed on to the police. These messages came from far and wide. One message said that April was behind someone's fireplace. One message mentioned something being boarded up. I had one message in particular that said that the psychic who'd written to me had a picture of a white cottage and a fire in their mind when they thought of where April might be. Others also told me about a white house. One description sounded very much like a building that I was familiar with in Machynlleth and I told the police this. They checked it out, but there was nothing there. They acted on the specific descriptions that were in these messages, especially ones that said very similar things.'

Alyson Jones was in no way frightened or puzzled by the messages that were being sent to her. She has no previous experience of psychics and mediums. She read each correspondence carefully before passing them on to the police.

'I am very open-minded about all this I have to say. I could tell that those who did get in touch with me were sincere and genuine and were doing what they thought was the helpful thing to do. In the desperate times such as we were facing, nothing is impossible, nothing is out of the question. I reacted to those offers of help with the same gratitude I would have shown if April was my child. We all went to the church service in October, whether we were churchgoers or not, ordinarily. That was pretty much about showing unity, which did involve showing that petty differences melt away at such times and the fact of whether we went to church or not, whether we believed in God or not, wasn't the issue. We were pulled there that day.'

The parish vicar Kathleen Rogers was in an extremely rare situation. Everyone in her parish was grieving at the same time. She was very much aware that all were grieving together, whether they went to her church, or to any church, or not. Locally she inevitably has had to face questions about the role of God in the light of such an evil event – and this from people she knows and sees daily. She was asked this in a television interview too. A few months later, she reflected on that same question.

'I quite simply have to say with all honesty that we do not understand what has happened. There are no ready answers. But I am equally convinced that God is here, in Mach. I wouldn't have been able to do what I've had to do for months on end if God hadn't been with me. People who have known me since I was a child can't believe that I have managed to fulfill the role I was thrust into. Even being a parish vicar, I am not one for the public eye. God has given me every word I have said. And, hard as it is to comprehend, I know that God was with April when she went through whatever she went through. That's the hope we have to stand on, not hang on to, but stand on.'

As well as facing such questions and wrestling with spiritual dilemmas, Kathleen Rogers and the people in her town have shared in other ways too.

'We've cried a lot. We've cried together, at the side of the road or wherever we have been overcome with the sense of grief. We've also hugged a lot. There's a lot of comfort in a hug and, quite often, that's all that was needed. No wise sayings, no platitudes, no verses from the Bible, no words at all, just putting our arms firmly and reassuringly around each other.'

7

We can't all
search for little April

As THE DAYS turned to weeks, messages started to pour into Machynlleth from other parts of Wales and the UK, as well as from many countries around the world. Letters and emails came from those concerned for April, her family, the community of Machynlleth and community leaders. This kind of response is nothing new, of course. People from places far removed from the locality of a particular tragedy often respond by sending messages to the people involved. It happened at Aberfan, Hungerford, Lockerbie and far too many other places. In Soham, for example, Kevin Wells has many entries in his diary-based book about the taking of his daughter, which refer to the mail coming in large quantities to their home.

Letters sent to Machynlleth offered sympathy and support to April's family and many noted that the writer had been encouraged by the way the people of Machynlleth had responded to April's abduction. They were heartened that there were more good people than evil ones. Many wrote that they had lit a candle in their church to symbolise their hope for April's wellbeing, and later in remembrance of April. Many churches throughout the UK burnt candles through the dark winter months. Others wrote that pink ribbons had been distributed, worn and displayed in their areas. Some people expressed their desire to visit Machynlleth to pay their respects to the family and the community. Some letters included donations and offered specific support and encouragement to people like Kathleen Rogers as she undertook her challenging role.

Many of these cards and letters were sent by post, of course. But whereas the bulk of communications with the families in Soham were by letter, Machynlleth was different. Some messages were emailed to various community leaders in the town. Both the speed with which the majority of the messages arrived and the manner they arrived, made the response to this particular story a social media-inspired one. We've heard already how many of the hundreds who turned up soon after April's disappearance were there having seen the news on Facebook. That particular social media platform also turned out to be the main medium of response for other people who, 'couldn't all search for April'.

The 'Help Find Missing 5-year-old April Jones' page on Facebook has been 'liked' by more than 178,000 and nearly 20,000 'conversations' have been held on that page. 'Find April Jones' Facebook page has more than 25,000 'likes'; the 'R.I.P. April Jones' page has more than 54,000 likes and 500 'conversations' on it. Some R.I.P. sites were 'live' before it had yet been confirmed that April had actually died. This upset the parents considerably and these sites were removed.

Yet another site, 'Search for April Jones x Missing 5 year old' was set up on 1 October, but was no longer active by November. It shows 342 'likes' for the first few weeks after April's disappearance. Another site was set up called 'April Jones Pink Ribbon Profile Picture', in order to encourage people to use images related to April as their own personal profile picture on Facebook.

There might well be overlaps from one site to the other, meaning that some of those counted on one page might also be on the others. But even allowing for that, and noting the fact that there were many from Machynlleth and the Dyfi Valley among those numbers too, the response from people from outside the area can be counted in many tens of thousands.

But, however many thousands used this particular platform,

the content of the message was very similar in nature. Firstly, overwhelming messages of support and prayer, and secondly, the disseminating of information. Each development in the investigation and the search was spread through Facebook and Twitter, with many updates happening throughout any given day.

One of those most actively involved with the use of Facebook in the unfolding story is Beckah Emma-Jayne Pughe. In her 20s, she hails from mid Wales but lived in Canterbury last October. She heard through social media that April had disappeared and was soon in touch with her friends and family back in Wales to find out more. Her sister Rosie started a page on Facebook immediately to keep people in touch with developments and to spread the word in the hope that April would be found. Rosie, however, had a little boy of her own and felt it too difficult to carry on with such a page in such circumstances. Beckah then took over the running of the Facebook page, 'Find April Jones'.

'I saw the story on the news and it became so real and horrible to see a town so close to home in the middle of such a story, and then of course to think of Paul and Coral and the rest of the family. It was horrendous. I really wanted to do something, but I was so far away. My sister not being able to carry on with the Facebook page gave me the opportunity I was looking for.'

Beckah had seen April on the Bryn y Gog estate a few times, as she has acquaintances who live on the estate whose children used to play with April. Setting up 'Find April Jones' put Beckah right at the heart of the story even though she was in the south of England. She was soon extremely busy.

'The first response was two-fold really. We obviously didn't know everything the police knew and there wasn't much on the news at those early stages. I suppose they were waiting to know some more detail before getting involved. So we were an information service for a long time. People would send whatever they knew in to me and I would then put it on the

Facebook page. Bits of the story were coming in, in dribs and drabs, and a picture was forming of what was happening in Mach. We had to face questions we didn't know answers to, so we had to answer each other. A lot of it was contradictory, of course, so I had to filter what was coming in quite a bit.

'The other role was spreading the message of Hope that was so strong and prominent in Mach itself. We were being sent pictures of ribbons in various places, and other ways that people kept April's name in the public eye. They were sent to my inbox and I would post them.'

Beckah was helped by Marrisa O'Hara and Arawn Sion Thompson, both from the Machynlleth area. Messages were soon coming in from all over the world, and Australia in particular. The site received hundreds of posts. One woman got in touch to say that she had found a pink balloon in her garden in south Wales, one that had been released in Machynlleth. The Facebook page played a role in an early public showing of solidarity with April.

'A big sign was placed on a hill above the town, with the name Machynlleth in bold pink letters, Hollywood style. It wasn't a very stable structure and there were calls to take it down on the page. I didn't feel that was possible without asking Paul and Coral first, so I contacted them to ask if they minded us taking it down. They had no objection, so down it came. That was the first time I had spoken to them since April was taken.'

But with spreading information, photographs and hope, came the darker side of social media. Beckah found that she had to filter quite a lot of unsavoury material.

'For some sick reason, some people were far too keen to say things that were derogatory and nasty. Some doubted if Paul was her father. Some said that there was nothing wrong with April and that the details of an illness were added to increase the sympathy. Others went further and said that Paul and Coral just couldn't cope with a child that needed so much attention and that they were the ones behind what happened to her. Some blamed Coral and Paul for letting April go out to play and said it was their fault. There were very upsetting and hurtful things said, without a doubt. None of these things were put on Facebook, we kept them away and concentrated on the good things.'

The Facebook page, 'Find April Jones' is still going, run predominantly by Beckah and Arawn Sion Thompson, with contributions from Marrisa. They still put stories related to April on it, but are in the process of changing its name.

The websites of many organisations got involved with the debate surrounding April's story, from football websites, the Caravan Club website, Mumsnet and online bingo, all examples showing how a virtual community got in touch. One entry on a Facebook page, written by Tony Marsland after the trial, reads like this:

'I'm posting this message just to let you know that I run a bingo group on Facebook with over 3,000 members from around the world. Every member of my group showed our respect and remembrance towards Coral and Paul and the family and all had a 2 mins silence where each and every member reflected what you have been through, and all send their deepest wishes to you all. This has been a real, harrowing time and justice has now been done, but April's memory will live on throughout the bingo community on Facebook and will continue to remember her; may God be with you now and hope the justice which has been served may help in some way to help you, God bless.'

There were many similar messages on various Facebook pages. It's only recently that the role of social media in the process of public grieving has been researched and the Machynlleth example will no doubt be subject to fuller analysis in time. But it is true to say that the increased access to a plethora of digital tools has given us a new way to react to death and grief. One academic publication, *Health Sociology Review*, sums up the situation in this way:

'Through the internet, people are increasingly making their lives, experiences, and bodies open to public viewing, comment and consumption. There is a vast archive of virtual cemeteries, memorials, grief chat rooms, grief blogs, and condolence messages on the worldwide web. Beyond more traditional and/ or government based forms of acknowledging a life and a death, for example, birth and death certificates and announcements of births and deaths in newspapers, new forms of technology have created a form of do-it-yourself (DIY) rites of mourning and memorialisation.'

April's story is the clearest example we have had in the UK of this DIY rite of mourning through social media following a tragedy.

But it is not unquestioningly accepted that this digital grieving is actually a source of good. Many wonder whether this way of responding to death is appropriate. Many still feel it inappropriate to comment so publicly on a personal tragedy, however public all forms of media have actually made that tragedy. One example, by a student at the University of Kansas, following a specific tragedy known to her, sums it up in this way: '... I felt that it was not necessary to say anything on their page, after all, I probably would not have written something on that day if they were alive, so why should I get to share in the grief of those close to these people now that they aren't?'

Some in Machynlleth expressed similar feelings, saying it was not right to comment so openly on such a private grief. This choice to keep grief as private as possible showed itself in another completely unrelated way in Machynlleth as well. Lately people have told shopkeepers and restaurant staff in the town that they had stayed away from Machynlleth for the best part of the last year because they 'didn't want to interfere' or 'they didn't want to disturb people'.

Other reservations turn on the fact that, on a mass public platform, not everyone is going to be at the same level of friendship or understanding and therefore the nature of any support or benefit on offer has to be questioned.

But, to quote Chris Syme, the author of recently published *Practice Safe Social* based on the developing role of social media in our world: 'Whether we like it or not, social media has become a public stage for human emotion. Facebook, Twitter and other mediums offer a valuable medium for people looking to express sorrow, grief, anger, and every emotion in between. And the channel fosters an environment of community that allows people to feel that they are all together in one big room. Scary and fantastic all at the same time.'

There are now websites dedicated to offer guidelines as to how to grieve on Facebook and Twitter. They include numerous examples of such grieving in the light of incidents similar to April's murder and the death of celebrities such as Whitney Houston. They also offer help to anyone interested in arranging reaction to their own death on a social media platform.

Those who embrace social media see it filling a very specific gap, one left by the declining influence of traditional religious belief. Bruce Feiler, in the *New York Times*, puts it this way: 'Grieving has been largely guided by religious communities, from celebratory Catholic wakes, to the 49 days of mourning for Buddhists, to the wearing of black (or white) in many Protestant traditions, to the week-long in-house condolence gatherings that make up the Jewish tradition of Shiva. Today, with religiosity in decline, families dispersed and the pace of life feeling quickened, these elaborate, carefully staged mourning rituals are less and less common. Old customs no longer apply, yet new ones have yet to materialise.'

He then goes on to say how social media is an example of the new customs materialising: 'Facebook presents its own challenges. The site's public platform is an ideal way to notify a large number of people, and many grievers I know have taken comfort in supportive messages from friends. Like CaringBridge, CarePages and similar sites, social networks can become like virtual Shiva locations for faraway loved ones.'

Social media then is the platform for grieving in a secular age, where the way we react to death is not shaped or defined by credo but by the virtual. Despite the doubts and uncertainties, social media will play an increasingly prominent role in dealing with stories such as April's. In Machynlleth itself, the mourning rituals were far more traditional, as we have already seen in the church service held on that Sunday morning. But, on a wider scale, social media proved to offer a service of its own. It's not only academics who are seeing this tendency. Practitioners in grief counselling are beginning to see its use as well. Kristie West is a grief specialist:

'Collective grief can happen on a much larger and much more open scale through social media. Sharing thoughts and feelings with millions of people around the world can now be easily done with social media, which also provides a platform for interaction between them. In response to such deaths and disaster, solidarity and support are often shown through a formation of Facebook groups, as an example, bringing a community connection.'

On another more practical level, the use of Facebook proved to be both a problem and a blessing for the emergency and rescue services back in October. Because word about April's disappearance got out so quickly on Facebook, hundreds gathered within a very short time at the Leisure Centre. Consequently, when the police and rescuers arrived, they not only had their own operation to coordinate, but they had a crowd to deal with too.

'We weren't ready for that,' says Mark Jones of the Brecon Mountain Rescue team. 'There's no way we had faced such a situation before and Facebook had a large part to play in that. It took a while longer then to set things up because of that additional factor.'

It might well have been a challenge on that first day of October, but since then Mark Jones says that they have taken on board some of the lessons learned at Machynlleth.

'Since that search and rescue operation, we have started to use Twitter and some of the other social media sites ourselves. We have found that using the sites of people local to an incident we have been called to is extremely useful to gauge a situation before we get there. It's been a positive development for us.'

Auctions were held on many online sites to raise money for

April's Fund, with eBay being the most popular. One rather unusual example of items auctioned makes use of the growing American trend of reborn baby dolls. According to Wikipedia, 'a reborn doll is a manufactured vinyl doll that has been transformed to resemble a human baby with as much realism as possible'.

The process involves taking the manufactured vinyl doll apart and removing all paint, then a blue colourwash is applied to the inside of each vinyl part to give the appearance of realistic baby skin undertones. For dolls with an awake appearance eyes must be replaced. The outer layer of the vinyl doll is given its skin tone by adding dozens of layers of flesh-coloured paint. The process continues until the doll, or the 'reborn' as it then is, looks as much like a human as it is possible for it to be. As well as the use of such dolls for purely play purposes, there are many therapeutic and emotional reasons why people get in to 'reborning' or buy 'reborns'. They are often used to simulate adoption; mothers who've miscarried turn to them as a comforting replacement. One such doll was sold for £75 on eBay, with the money going to April's Fund. The unnamed person who made the doll explains her reasons for doing so, which includes reference to the fact that the doll was intended to be a girl but it turned out to look more like a boy:

> Say hello to a very special beautiful baby boy... to anyone that is thinking of adopting this little gem, you will be buying a reborn and all the money will go to Coral and Paul Jones, for them to buy something that April loved or something that will be remembered or help toward something else. I have their consent to use their names and little April's name in this listing and will also be giving them the item number for this.

But without a doubt, the most high-profile and visible symbol of April's story was the pink bow. It was an idea instigated by April's mum Coral, based on the fact that pink was her daughter's favourite colour. She was at pains to emphasise, in conversation with the author, that the ribbon was to be tied in a full bow, and not the loop that was often seen in the early days. It had to be the bow, she said, not to be mistaken with the breast cancer pink loop. The pink ribbon idea started with three ribbons tied onto the gate at the front of April's home on the Bryn y Gog estate by her mother. She then appealed through Facebook for others to use the pink ribbon as an act of continued hope, adding the words, 'Please keep looking for April, she needs to come home.' That was on 4 October.

The full pink bow soon took hold in the public imagination and nowhere more so, of course, than in Machynlleth town centre. By the end of the first day that Coral had chosen the pink bow as a symbol of hope that April was alive and well, Machynlleth was draped in pink bows. It was, as the *Daily Mail* said, 'an extraordinary act of solidarity'.

Following Coral's request to wear pink ribbons, Wheeler's haberdashery and drapers' shop in Machynlleth had sold hundreds of ribbons within a couple of hours. The shop's owner, Sam Wheeler, said that he ran out of every bit of pink fabric before the day was out. In having to meet the demand for the ribbons, Wheeler's had to put its usual business to one side. Again, as in other businesses and with other individuals, there was a strong feeling in that shop that to carry on as normal would actually be wrong.

Another local businessman played his part in spreading the ribbon symbol too and, as at Wheeler's, his normal business was put to one side as well. About a week into the ribbon campaign, El Diablo's tattoo shop in the middle of Machynlleth town centre was inundated with requests for pink ribbon tattoos. Owner Rob, known as Rambo locally, was one of those involved in the search on that very first day, having called his wife, who was on a night out, back home so that she could look after the children as he went out looking. He cancelled his bookings for three days in order to keep searching. A week later, he felt the need to help in another way.

'Once the pink ribbon thing took off, it became obvious that many didn't just want to pin one to their clothes but wanted them tattooed to parts of their body. That interest grew steadily as the first week since her disappearance went on. So I then set a day aside to do nothing but tattoo pink bows on people. There was an overwhelming response and I was lucky that a fellow tattoo artist mate of mine had come down from north Wales to help me out for the day.'

Rob and his friend tattooed either the pink bow or the word 'Hope' on more than 40 people, raising £1,300 for Paul and Coral. He was insistent that the money went directly to the couple and not to the fund that was beginning to gather momentum at the time.

'I didn't doubt the fund or anything; I just knew that Paul and Coral would need money there and then. I didn't think there was any point in them waiting until things were set in motion properly, so I sent it straight away.'

Among the customers in El Diablo's that week were Paul and Coral, Paul's father and Paul's other daughter. They had the pink bow tattoo as well.

'I've known Paul and Coral for a while, and I knew Mark Bridger too. I tattooed him years ago and at one time, where I lived, Paul and Coral lived a few doors down and Bridger lived round the back of us.'

The demand for pink bows or 'hope' tattoos has understandably slowed down over the last months. But it hasn't disappeared.

'I've tattooed 'hope' a few times this month (August 2013) and a couple called in recently who were on holiday in the area. They wanted a pink ribbon done while they were in the town because they were affected by the story so much. A lot of holidaymakers have called in over the months, wanting tattoos done here because it is where the story happened. They also said they felt that any money they might donate while they were here would be more certain to go to the fund as they were closer to the source.'

Tourists wanting the 'authentic' Machynlleth pink bow tattoo in the town itself is the closest that the townspeople have come to what's described as grief tourism – the practice of specifically visiting an area where a tragedy has happened in order to see the main places associated with that tragedy. Belfast and Beirut are two cities that have been on the receiving end of such a phenomenon, both being must-see cities for those who want to visit areas of tragedy, disaster or war. Some simply call it dark tourism. The best, or worst example, again takes us to Soham. Following the murders of Jessica Chapman and Holly Wells, the town did receive thousands of well-wishing visitors. But in their midst, and for a while after the verdict, were those who went there to see where Ian Huntley lived, the school where he was a caretaker and where Maxine Carr lived. Coach companies who were taking tourists to nearby Ely Cathedral made a deliberate detour to go through Soham. One story tells of a couple who put up deckchairs in the church graveyard and were eating fish and chips there. Machynlleth, as has already been intimated, has actually seen the reverse. Coach companies did not stop in the town for a long time after October. The town is on the north/south route and a stop in Machynlleth would be customary enough.

'It was terrible for a while,' says one local businessman. 'We thought things were quiet and then we got word that the coach companies were not stopping here. Visitors didn't come here for a while but, of course, we respect the fact that they were only thinking of us.'

'It was actually the opposite of what we wanted,' says another shop owner, 'which was for people to carry on coming and keep the town going. We needed the normal routine. It took a while, but it's back now, thank goodness.'

Ribbon or bow wearing is a relatively recent sign of individuals identifying with a cause or an incident. Beginning in 1991 with the red Aids ribbon, this later custom of wearing ribbons or bows comes from the tradition of poppy wearing on Remembrance Day and the more recent American tradition of tying a yellow ribbon round a tree. In recent years, there have been ribbons for breast cancer, the Oklahoma bombing, male violence, censorship, bullying, epilepsy, diabetes, ME, autism, racial abuse, childhood disability, mouth cancer, and so on. The colours vary – blue could be for Internet censorship or mouth cancer, green could be for Tourette's or ovarian cancer, purple for the homeless or Alzheimer's.

Of all the examples, the vast majority are either for a medical condition or a social cause. Very few are for tragedies such as April's. In her book *Ribbon Culture*, Sarah E H Moore says: 'Ribbon wearing has become an increasingly visible aspect of our social reality, a form of mass participation in a society that is otherwise experiencing a decline in other forms of such activity.'

Those other activities referred to are the various ways of being involved in civil society, with voting being the most obvious. This link with voting was also commented on by one psychoanalyst, Dr Michael Pokorny, in the *Daily Mail*. He made this comment in response to the public grief following the death of schoolgirl Sarah Payne:

'What is also interesting about this phenomenon is that it has arisen at a time when the number of people voting is falling, so this has become a way that people express themselves, possibly instead of voting. It becomes a political gesture. The gifts also become tributes, like a tribute to the gods, recognising that other people have been struck by tragedy instead of them; and a kind of talisman, with the hope that the person leaving the tribute will not be struck.'

How this relates to the wearing of the pink ribbons for April, again, will be a field of study in time to come. But there's no doubt that this practice, in the not-so-common context of a criminal incident yet alone child abduction and murder, again takes its place in a wider social trend, echoing poignantly as it does, the yellow ribbons for Madeleine McCann.

In Machynlleth, there were one or two dissenting voices who questioned the pink ribbon phenomena. They were a small minority, but the author's conversations with two individuals led to comments being made that pink ribbons were 'girlifying' or 'sexualising' the whole story and indeed going much further than that, saying that the use of such a symbol, in such a colour, was feeding the very mindset that triggers such predators as Mark Bridger. One noted that the colour of the ribbons changed as weeks went by, moving from a more baby pink to a much deeper pink, suggesting that this was a conscious decision because someone had become aware of the inappropriateness of baby pink. There's no evidence to suggest that this actually was the case.

In November, one unusual gesture of solidarity came from an unexpected source. The town council received a letter from inmates at HMP Shrewsbury saying that they had made a bench from oak recovered from the River Severn. They wanted to ask the council if the bench could be placed in the town centre as a permanent dedication to April.

This request touched the hearts of the councillors, as the then town clerk, Mel Biffin remarked. The letter notes: 'The bench has already been made and we would like to deliver and install it, together with an engraved plaque, in loving memory of this little girl who was so sadly taken from her beloved mother, father, family and friends... Again, may we offer our deepest condolences at this sad time.'

It wasn't possible to place the bench in the town centre, as the then mayor Gareth Jones explains: 'Pavements are owned by Powys County Council and, as a result, there would have been much more involvement in getting permission to put the bench there. It was easier for us to respond quicker. And there were also insurance issues and the like in such a busy town centre, it just wasn't an easy place to put it. So it was decided to put it in the grounds of Y Plas, in a lovely garden setting, in the shadow of where the police investigation was coordinated and the gathering point for the hundreds of volunteers.'

But, at the last minute, however, as plans were being made to unveil the bench at Y Plas, a request came from April's parents

116

for the bench to be placed on the Bryn y Gog estate. And that's where it is located alongside a footpath through the estate, in one of the three areas turned into gardens of remembrance for April, a few yards from her home.

April's story takes its place alongside other community responses to tragedies all over the world. It shows how the human spirit can respond in times of adversity. It shows us how we can be united by the dramatic, sudden taking of a life while, at the same time, raises questions about our attitude to death. It is the clearest example, to date, of the way that all forms of media can play their part in bringing us face-to-face with death.

The way we grieve in public has changed significantly over the years, with the reaction to the death of Diana a significant milestone. The outpouring of sympathy and grief shown at the time of both her death and funeral was unprecedented. But given the all-pervasiveness of the public reaction to stories such as Diana's death and others, as well as the reaction to death as the result of a crime or tragedy, there are those who strongly refute that mass mourning is a positive thing. The term mourning sickness is applied to such a reaction, with a clear indication that it actually a dis-ease if not an actual disease. A summary of this kind of reaction comes from Patrick West's book *Conspicuous Compassion*: '... such displays of empathy do not change the world for the better: they do not help the poor, diseased, dispossessed or bereaved. Our culture of ostentatious caring concerns rather, projecting one's ego, and informing others what a deeply caring individual you are. It is about feeling good, not doing good, and illustrates not how altruistic we have become, but how selfish.'

With specific reference to Soham, in an article in *The Irish Independent* in 2004, Gwen Halley is equally blunt in her condemnation of 'attaching our bogus grief onto the genuine grief of others':

'Grief on such a grand operatic scale is as fraudulent as a male boast. Prolonging grief and national mourning is a selfish, voyeuristic and unclean exercise. Would the millions of boo-hooing spectators who tuned into the Wells documentary have been interested if the girls had died in a car crash? We tuned into Soham for its cocktail of packaged evil. Murder and paedophilia with a heavy foam of promised recreational mourning. Sex and violence wrapped in moral outrage and shallow sorrow.'

The author then goes on to link such a reaction to events in Soham with the reaction to Diana's death.

'The grief bandwagon had moved from Kensington Palace to Soham. The Princess Diana catharsis had ended and the grief tourists boarded their coaches once again with their tears, tissues and pity picnics. We Irish funeral fanatics understand the close correlation between emoting and socialization. Nothing like a good cry and a hearty natter over soup and sandwiches to heal the mind. Pure grief therapy.'

Strong words indeed. And no doubt there might well be an element of truth in them in relation to a proportion of the wider reaction to April's story. But this story is child-centred. That strikes right at the core of our sense of vulnerability and innocence; something precious to our very being, something that should be untouched and untainted has been violated. This makes the reaction all the less likely to be mass hysteria or superficial. And parents would have a double response. Again, in response to the death of Sarah Payne, psychologist Helen Haste suggests that a horrific incident involving the death of a child does make the reaction different: 'People start thinking about their own families, and it touches people on a very personal level. And in the case of Sarah there was also the fact that her parents were visibly emoting in public, showing their grief and distress, and that would also have had an effect.'

But in Machynlleth itself, there was never any danger of anyone falling foul of the mourning sickness disease. There is a clear difference between the reaction at the heart of the community and that of those from far and wide. But no doubt that the majority who got in touch from afar, through new means or old, were standing side-by-side in genuine grief for April's family and Machynlleth citizens.

8

The pity and the poetry

AN INADEQUACY IN finding the correct words to say is a common reaction to bereavement. Grief is so often inexpressible. It may be deep-felt but, nonetheless, it is so often not possible to be articulated. This is certainly true of grief following a killing such as April's. This has been the experience of many in Machynlleth. But finding a way for those feelings to be externalised is also something some people have to do, however difficult it might be. Talking, sharing, going for counselling might not be possible. But some thing, some way, some method has to be found to channel the grief, the sorrow, the anger, the bitterness, whatever the dominant feeling is in the individual.

The service held at St Peter's Church on that Sunday in October was an early way of giving people the chance to express what they had experienced, even if it was only walking arm-in-arm through the streets of their home town. The service included Kathleen Rogers reading two poems – creative expressions of two themes at the heart of the town's tragedy, motherhood and childhood. The first addressed Coral, April's mum.

Mum
She's a:
Sadness Stealer
Cut-knee healer
Hug-me-tighter
Wrongness righter
Gold star carer
Chocolate sharer (well, sometimes!)

Hamster feeder
Bedtime reader
Great game player
Night fear slayer
Treat dispenser
Naughty sensor (how come she always knows?)
She's my
Never glum,
Constant chum
Second to none
We're under her thumb!
Mum!

Polly Peters

The second poem read out in the service echoed the many messages sent in since then, mainly on Facebook, offering phrases such as April now being an Angel in Heaven, with God in Heaven, in a better place – all alluding to a belief in a safe afterlife, where there's no pain and suffering. Such words offer comfort and putting it in poetry form is all part of that process too, as rhythm and rhyme offer solace.

There's a Friend for little children
Above the bright blue sky,
A Friend who never changes
Whose love will never die;
Our earthly friends may fail us,
And change with changing years,
This Friend is always worthy
Of that dear name he bears.

There's a home for little children
Above the bright blue sky,
Where Jesus reigns in glory,
A home of peace and joy;
No home on earth is like it,
Nor can with it compare;
And everyone is happy, nor could be happier there.

Albert Midlane (1859)

After that service many chose to put their thoughts and feelings about April in poetry form. In recent times, the most populist response to 9/11 was the release of Bruce Springsteen's album, *The Rising*, in which one track, 'My City of Ruins', contains the rousing chant, 'Come on, rise up!' In another instance, author Haruki Murakami wrote a collection of short stories after the earthquake in Kobe, Japan, in 1995 called *After the Quake*, a book dubbed by one reviewer as '... Murakami's deeply felt get well card.' It was also one of the ways that Kevin Wells responded to the taking of his own daughter. Never having written a poem before, he felt the need to put pen to paper in memory of the daughter he'd just lost. He called his work 'Soham's Rose'.

Your right to grow, to mature, and to play
So cruelly denied, in a sinister way.
Attentive and caring, a parent's delight
But so young at heart, needing comfort at night.

The garden is quiet, the house is too,
But pausing for a moment, we can still sense you.
Your trusting nature and desire to please all
Allow us, your family, to remain walking tall.

Our memories, now shared, with the Nation's hearts
Small crumbs of comfort, now it's time to part.
We will never forget you, Heaven's gain, as it knows
Is simply you Holly, our beautiful Soham Rose.

Kevin Wells

One of the first to respond in such a manner to April's story was the National Poet of Wales, Gillian Clarke. She sent a specially written poem to Machynlleth called, simply, 'Daughter'.

A pearl, April, born of water,
borne now in the river's arms,
child of the mountain,
mermaid of the estuary,
everyone's daughter.
Let her not be lost to the mothering sea.
Let her be light on the wave.
Let her change us forever.
Let us see her sweet face whenever
we gaze on the river, the sea,
like the moon on water.
Let this pain that is sleepless
lighten to love, to kindness.
Let ours be the arms that caught her,
Love's weight, her light, the lightness
of everyone's daughter.

Gillian Clarke

In answer to why she felt the need to write a poem, this is what she said to the author: 'What a task, to describe the hurt and confusion of a whole community, and of the family at the heart of it, whose agony can only be imagined. I admire those people so much, and am proud of their dignity and restraint. I wrote the poem because, as National Poet, I thought I should put into words what we all felt. I wrote it on behalf of our people, thinking of all our children. I held back for a while because I was torn between poetic duty and the need to avoid exploiting the tragedy, and adding to anyone's pain. Then the poem arrived in my head in a few minutes, while the fields and mountains and mines around Machynlleth were full of searchers, long before we knew April was dead. I held on to it for a while, and eventually sent it to the vicar to do as she thought best, because she seemed compassionate and sensible. I have no idea if April's parents have seen it, but I would like them to know that I expressed something the whole nation felt, that their hurt was important, that we cared. I wanted that child to be remembered forever. She will be, of course, with or without my poem.'

But, as with the Facebook response, not all think that putting feelings down in poetic form is an appropriate response to tragedy. Again, with reference to 9/11, the question asked by many in light of creative projects in response to what happened that day, was, quite simply, 'How dare the arts attempt to minister to such horror, emptiness and tragedy?' The most famous expression of such a way of thinking is that made by Theodor Adorno when he argued in his 1949 essay 'Cultural Criticism and Society', 'To write poetry after Auschwitz is barbaric'.

But Gillian Clarke had no such reservations. The tragedies themselves might vary in both scale and consequence, but the same human need is touched by each: 'Wilfred Owen said the poetry is in the pity. There is no doubt that we turn to an appropriate poem for consolation or affirmation, if one presents itself. The sudden popularity of Auden's 'Stop all the Clocks', used in the film *Four Weddings and a Funeral* is proof of that. The right published words on the great emotions, love, loss, grief, affirm our shared humanity.

'It is entirely appropriate if the event "belongs" to you. I live 40 miles away, and am often in or passing through Machynlleth. I have many friends there. I would not write about distant tragedies, where the pain belongs to others, and we only feel a faint echo of that hurt. That is exploitation. This was different. It is personal. It was our hurt, our community, our responsibility, in the whole of Ceredigion, and of Wales too. That is shown by the way the farmers led searches of their own land, people I know went down old mine-shafts. They could not be stopped from turning up to help the police, and the police had to manage that situation. Machynlleth is close, real, and I have, in the past, worked with the children of Machynlleth giving poetry workshops. April is everyone's daughter.

'I only noted one man who shouted, banged the police van with the accused inside and called for bringing back hanging, and he came from Birmingham. Mach, and the whole of west Wales, behaved with dignified restraint.'

While the people of Machynlleth were waiting cocooned in that dignified restraint, one voice reached out to them from an area of Scotland that had known its own grief and tragedy, Dunblane. Ruth Burgess lives in that town and is a member of the Iona Community, a dispersed Christian ecumenical community. The author describes her work more as a prayer than a poem. Copies were displayed in the church in Machynlleth as well as in some shops.

Waiting

In quiet and in sadness
We wait
With questions and anger
We wait
With friends and with family
We wait
We wait and we cry 'How Long'?

In the morning and the evening
We wait
As the world goes on around us
We wait
With an emptiness inside us
We wait
We wait and we cry 'How Long'?

With the town of Machynlleth
We wait
With our children and our neighbours
We wait
With all who are sad and exhausted
We wait
We wait and we cry 'How Long'?

Ruth Burgess

'Waiting' was a key word for all affected by the news of April's disappearance and 'waiting' turned out to have a heavier significance when the word 'abduction' was then added to the story. With the passing of time, and still no sign of finding April, waiting became a way of life, an attitude, a way of feeling. This prayer spoke right to the heart of Machynlleth's waiting people, and Paul and Coral. In explaining why she wrote 'Waiting', Ruth Burgess says that it was the result of the Iona Community keeping in close touch with developments in Machynlleth.

'We kept in close touch with what was going on there as the terrible tragedy unfolded. It was so terrible to think of everyone, especially the family, of course, waiting for news all the time, from hour-to-hour at first, then from day-to-day and week-to-week. Their days were days of questions and not answers. That is still true to a large extent, of course, but it was particularly true and raw in those early days. I wondered how people get on with day-to-day life in the midst of all the waiting. Although I call it a prayer, and it is just that, it doesn't mention God at all. They are thoughts that are open to all.'

The place where the poem was written adds an additional poignancy; that community too went through so much pain when many of its children's lives were taken when Thomas Hamilton shot and killed 16 children in 1996.

Susan Dale responded to that prayer by saying that, 'It comforts us that others are standing alongside. Now with the trial well underway, we are beginning to get answers; perhaps not the answers we wanted to hear, but our waiting is finally coming towards an end.'

Many poems appeared online and were written especially for April. One such example is by Shar: 'I've started a new topic on this tragic story. If anyone would care to show their respect, please feel free. We can't all search for little April but we are praying and desperately hoping that she is alive and well. Although, it doesn't appear to be that way, we never know. As

I said, none of us know what is to be next. Say a prayer, poem, or just what you 'feel'. Thank you. Shar.'

April-like the showers April the month brings,

our emotions pour over us, our hearts are filled with sorrow when all we wish for is that song Bird who sings.

A sign, a place where they find you safe is the only thing that keeps our sanity for you, a little flower so beautiful and so brave. What else can we say or do?

No child should be taken.

Is the man in custody guilty, or are they mistaken?

So many questions in our mind and in our heart, it tears us up beyond belief

no escape, as you still haven't been found, not any much needed relief.

We start to suspect other people, but everyone should have wished you nothing but being kept safe.

Sniffer dogs and search teams looking everywhere in a big bad world such a tiny little girl – you might be anywhere.

Wherever you are I hope you're not in pain

and that God or another force will bring you back again.

She could be miles and miles away from the place,

and never found

if they did not stop off with her locally.

Dear God I pray so hard that this doesn't go on for any longer.

To April and her family, loved ones and friends.

We think about you constantly.

God Bless

Shar

Another was written by someone by the name of Bristol Boy; it was called 'Hear Us Calling Out to You'.

We know you're out there somewhere,
So afraid and all alone.
But hear us calling out to you,
To guide you safely home.

We know that you are frightened,
We know that you are scared.
But walk towards our voices,
We are people here that care.

Be brave my little princess,
Just listen out for our gentle tone.
For each and every single voice,
Is guiding you back home.

Listen to our voices,
Try with all your might.
If you have difficulties following them,
Look for our candle lights.

They will guide you home my darling,
Don't be afraid I promise thee.
Follow our voices and lit candles,
To the arms of your family.

Many of the poems on Facebook refer to April as the 'Little Welsh Princess' or 'Our Own Welsh Princess'. Many more refer to her as an 'Angel' or as 'Pretty Eyes'.

Others chose to find the creative in their grief in different ways. On another popular website, YouTube, many showed that April and her family were very much in their minds when creating videos to well-known songs. There are over a hundred such videos posted on YouTube, with images related to April's story added to them. The stars whose songs appear the most are Mariah Carey, Whitney Houston and Westlife. Others vary from Michael Bublé to Stooshe, Chicago to the Military Wives, Jerry Lee Lewis to Bryn Terfel and One Direction to Sinead O'Connor. The song titles have a common thread: 'Please

Remember', 'Carry your Candle', 'Gone too Soon', 'Tears in Heaven', 'Someone's Watching over Me', 'One Moment in Time', 'Somewhere Over the Rainbow', 'When You Believe', 'Miracles do Happen', 'Borrowed Angels', 'The Rose', 'The Greatest Love of All' and so on.

One video has an added significance. It was made by Sophie Lawrence, one of April's cousins. To the song 'The Prayer', which has been performed by Andrea Bocelli and Celine Dion, she has added many images of April. Family photos of happy occasions April enjoyed on outings to the beach, in the snow, playing, partying, dressing up and also at school. It's a fitting family tribute to a lost little girl. Words and music have played a large part in shaping the expression of grief, but other creative ways have been used too.

When Morlan, a centre for faith and culture in Aberystwyth, was holding one of its regular art exhibitions, a local photographer submitted a work relating to April's story. Iestyn Hughes was in the right place at the right time to capture a unique and poignant moment for a photographer. It was during the first week of October, the first time that lanterns were released into the sky as symbols of hope that April would be found alive:

'I was in my garden and I could see some lights up in the sky which looked rather unusual, but they had passed before I could take any shots of them. Then, a while later, there were more in the sky and this time I grabbed my camera. I could then see that they were lanterns. As I was holding it in front of my eyes ready to take photographs, some of them came right towards me and I was able to grab some shots relatively easy. They were, of course, some of the lanterns released to remember April.

'I'd been back and forth to Machynlleth for several days, either documenting the search, or delivering donations of food to the exhausted search teams. From what should have been a fairly simple request for a few photographs for a new news picture feed, I'd somehow been drawn into the events, and was becoming emotionally involved. After the Sunday procession from April's home to the local church, I decided to distance myself, and so I stayed home on Monday, deliberately avoiding the news.

'During the evening, as I sat by the kitchen table, my eye was drawn towards a light in the sky. I thought at first that it was a search helicopter but, as I stepped outside, I realised that there was no sound. It was a dark, silent night. The light which drifted quickly southwards turned and came directly towards me, so close that I felt that I could almost reach and touch it. A lantern. I remembered that April's family were going to light a lantern of hope for their little girl. I couldn't move, let alone take a picture. It was as if the lantern had diverted away from its course to confront me.

'Then, in a second or two, it rose up and headed back on its journey towards Aberystwyth. As it turned into a tiny speck, a second lantern appeared, much further away than the first, and I fetched the camera, raised it, took two rushed shots, then, feeling it imperative to get a picture, braced myself, calmly adjusted the settings, and took one last shot. And as I looked on, the lantern rose upwards and all of a sudden the light was extinguished.

'Something otherworldly had occurred, and I'll never forget the rush of emotion I felt as the lantern rose away from reach and sight.

'When asked to submit a picture to represent a poem at Aberystwyth's Morlan Centre Christmas exhibition, I felt that emotional surge once again when I read the outwardly simple poem by Tudur Dylan. My picture had found a purpose.'

The poem Iestyn used was 'Seren', which means star. It was written by Tudur Dylan Jones, one of Wales's foremost Welsh-language poets. It was not specifically written in response to April's disappearance, as poet Tudur Dylan Jones explains:

'This is a Christmas poem, composed in celebration of the stars above us. In the poem, somebody, somewhere, is in the darkness looking for the light, one small star in the deepest night, one small star to guide and comfort.

'It may be only a tiny speck of light, but sometimes the smallest flicker can be more powerful than all the light in the world.'

The words of the poem take on a new significance in its use by Iestyn Hughes in the context of April's story.

Seren

Mae'n hwyr y dydd dan yr awyr ddu,
ac mae rhywrai ar ddi-hun
yn chwilio'r nos am seren fach,
am y golau lleiaf un.

Y golau lleia fyth i wneud
y galon fach yn llawn,
un arwydd bychan bach i ddweud
fod popeth am fod yn iawn.

Un arwydd fod y wawr ar ddod
i wneud y byd yn well,
i godi calon un fel fi
ar ddiwedd taith mor bell.

Mae'n hwyr y dydd dan yr awyr ddu,
ac mae rhywrai ar ddi-hun,
yn gwybod mai'r golau lleiaf oll
yw'r golau mwyaf un.

Tudur Dylan

That framed photograph has been presented to Paul and Coral by Iestyn Hughes, along with a rough translation made by him of the accompanying poem. When he called at their house give it to them, reference was made in conversation to a 'Hugging Tree' and Iestyn said that he didn't know anything about it. Paul Jones then offered to take him up to it.

'After quite a steep walk nearly to the top of the hill overlooking the town of Machynlleth, I saw an amazing sight.

In a wooded area, one tree was dressed in pink, knitted and crochet patchwork squares embraced the tree from the ground to the higher branches. Some ribbons have been pinned on these squares, at random, and messages of hope and support written on them. It was a breathtaking sight to say the least. The whole area around the tree has a quiet, peaceful aura. It's quite special.'

While they were there, two holidaymakers from the Midlands approached the tree, obviously not having seen it before. They turned to Iestyn and Paul to ask if it was anything to do with April Jones. Without letting on who he was, Paul confirmed that it was one of the responses to what happened to April and that it was called the 'Hugging Tree'.

'The two men then went on to say that they were also on holiday in Machynlleth in October with their families, and when they heard what had happened to April, they took time out from their holiday to join in the search. When Paul heard this, he then said who he was and thanked them very much for giving up their free time and helping in October. They then stayed there a while after we left, in quiet contemplation.'

The Hugging Tree has grown in its significance over the last few months. But it shares the role of being a place of remembrance, contemplation and solace with another place more central to April's tragedy. On the grassy area outside her home a garden has been made. In fact, there are now three areas of garden, one rectangular where the prisoners' bench now sits and two circular ones behind it – one of these made around a tree that was already there and there's a newly-planted tree in the other. It's no surprise that the predominant colour is pink once again. The gardens have been generously planted, and blue and pink Bill and Ben flowerpot men sit guarding a raised planter. In the circular garden where the new tree has been planted, colourful butterflies and windmills give their own lift and lightness to the area. In the second circular garden, the tree has pink ribbons wrapped around it. Teddy bears, one big, cuddly pink one and three or four smaller ones, look out over all corners of Bryn y Gog, keeping their beady eyes specifically on the children who still live and play there.

A lot of time and effort has gone into creating these gardens and they are the result of another effort to express creatively reactions to something destructive. The end result is colour from darkness, order from chaos and beauty from ugliness.

In writing of the way the arts were used in the aftermath of 9/11, Naj Wikoff, the president of the Society for the Arts and Healthcare, says in the *ArtsLinks* publication:

'The terrorists used very simple things like matte knives to cause great destruction. We too can use very simple things like tape, pencils, crayons, a song, movement and yes, matte knives, to help the healing process, to bring light into this terrible darkness.'

In Machynlleth, wool, flowers, verse, photographs, songs, videos and trees can be added to that list. One short line from a poet, not linked to April's story, captures what creative expressions such as those noted here in Machynlleth, show. As Theodore Roetke says: 'In a dark time, the eyes begin to see...'

One of the most instinctive ways of expressing how creative we are as human beings was missing from Bryn y Gog for quite some time after 1 October. Children stopped playing outside in the way they used to. An estate full of homes for families and children fell silent as children's laughter, screaming and shouting disappeared – kept indoors by worried parents. But the children are back out now and, where they play, they see three areas of garden reminding them of what happened to one of their friends and offering hope in the world they now live in without her.

9

How will we ever get over it?

AFTER THE INITIAL news of April's disappearance, the first significant milestone happened the following Thursday when the police informed everyone that the search was now solely in their hands, implying that they thought there was little chance of finding her alive.

The next milestone was the service on the following Sunday when the community started the process of united healing in the midst of grief and confusion. And whereas calendar events such as Halloween, Bonfire Night and Christmas came and went, albeit with a new poignancy and significance, the next milestone was the trial of Mark Bridger and its subsequent verdict.

At Bridger's first hearing in January, the date of the Crown Court case was decided. That was scheduled to be at the end of February, but on the opening day it was postponed for another two months. Therefore, at the end of April, Bridger finally stood in the dock and the world got its first opportunity to find out what had actually happened. Not all the questions in people's minds were answered but those which were proved to be upsetting, sickening and heart-wrenching. And that was just for the residents of Machynlleth and the general public. How the revelations affected Paul and Coral we shall never know.

Bridger was charged with the offences of abduction, murder and perverting the course of justice. The jury at Mold Crown Court took four hours and six minutes to find him guilty of all charges and he was subsequently sentenced to life in prison, with the stipulation that life meant life. He is now one of only

48 convicts in England and Wales who are serving whole-life prison terms, mass killer Rose West being among them. He will never be a free man again.

In reaching that verdict, the horror of what happened that day in October was revealed. It does not make easy reading. Bridger had been seen by many people in Machynlleth that Monday afternoon; he had appeared to be in a world of his own, on the edge, out of control. One witness had seen him wearing his camouflage trousers and walking past the garages on Bryn y Gog; he had, unusually, ignored social greetings from people he passed. It was said that this was 'strange' behaviour for such a normally sociable person.

After he lured April into his Land Rover, he sped away through a back lane. As a result of Bridger's lack of cooperation in terms of saying exactly what happened that night, the police can only suggest what they think happened. Their suggestions are based on significant forensic evidence and detailed profiling of Bridger during 13 police interviews after his arrest. The police believe that April was taken by Bridger, then sexually abused by him – either at a remote location he had driven to in his Land Rover, or back in his Ceinws cottage, Mount Pleasant. They then believe that he dismembered her body. It is possible that the sighting of him returning to his home at 8.30 on the Monday was in fact him returning from disposing of her body.

Once home he needed to destroy any potential evidence that could link him to the evil acts he'd just committed. He sterilised knives, including a burnt boning knife the police investigation uncovered. He'd done a thorough job of cleaning up.

But, at home that night, he was also texting on his mobile. He texted the woman who had dumped him that morning. Bridger's message is:

'I've just heard the news. Is everything OK with you?'
'Mine [her children] are OK. Back out now, though not slept.'

He also exchanged messages with the mother of two of his children. She told him that the police were looking for a light coloured van or a Land Rover.

'OK, right. I'm out.'

As that fateful day for April drew to a close, he sent one further text message to a female friend. She asked him if he had picked up his benefits that day.

'Yes. I got a bottle of wine and a box of cider. Good benefits.'

And then just before midnight, two final texts between him and his friend:

'Goodnight hon, hope you're OK. Sweet dreams.'
'Good night, yes, benefits sorted, I hope.'

But despite all his efforts to clean his house of all potential evidence, he hadn't succeeded in getting rid of the traces of blood that were found in the bathroom and hall, and that which had seeped through to the underside of the carpet in his living room. This was April's blood. Throughout police interviews, and during his three days in the dock, Bridger stuck to his defence that he had accidentally crushed April in a car accident and that he had forgotten what he'd done with the body. But the key element to mounting such a flimsy defence was that April had not been at his home. When confronted with this discrepancy in court, he said that images of lying April down in front of the fire had come to him in dreams.

Crucial evidence also included 17 pieces of bone found in the ash of the wood burner and one piece in the bath plughole. Forensic scientists were unable to extract DNA from what was found, but some experts suggested they could have come from a child's skull. Police don't believe April's whole body was burned, but believe that fragments of bone got into the fire and bath during the nearly-thorough clean-up. The police tell April's family that they believe these fragments of skull bone to be April's.

When it comes to the forensic analysis of Bridger's clothing, there was more damning evidence. Scientists could not discount or rule out the possibility that April had 'contributed DNA' to a sample taken from the inside of the crotch area of Bridger's tracksuit bottoms. After he was arrested, Bridger added to the significance of such evidence by saying that if April's DNA was found on his penis, it might well have got there if he had a wee while he was carrying her.

The senior policeman leading the investigation, Detective Superintendent Andy John, believes that April went into the cottage alive and was killed there, before being dismembered and her body parts scattered across parts of the Dyfi Valley. Bridger, as a former abattoir and forestry worker, would have had extensive personal knowledge of both. At the time of the trial, Andy John said:

'I think the body has been dismembered and various parts have been placed in different areas, possibly those remains would have been small and damaged. That's why we've had such difficulty locating them. We've got fast-flowing rivers close by. At the time this offence occurred the river was very high and we can't rule out that parts may have gone into the river; we can't rule out that parts could have been burned on the fire.'

Analysis of Bridger's vehicle showed that he had travelled 400 miles since his Land Rover had last been serviced, two weeks previously. This, along with the gap in his movements which cannot be accounted for on that Monday, suggests that he might well have been able to travel quite far away from Machynlleth to dispose of April's body. But Andy John is confident that this might actually not have been the case, based on research and advice given. He thinks that, '... it would all point towards him going to areas he was comfortable with.'

Bridger's main undoing was the evidence of one of April's best friends, a seven-year-old girl. This little girl had the seen the whole episode when April got into his Land Rover and was able to tell police clearly what she'd seen. A murderer was undone by the innocent account of a seven-year-old girl.

The girl had been spoken to within minutes of April being reported missing. The only police officer on duty in Machynlleth that evening, PC Fiona Evans, spoke to the girl at 7.37 p.m. The policewoman heard the full story of what had happened to April behind the garages of her home on Bryn y Gog estate. The account given by the seven-year-old turned out to be incredibly accurate.

The anxious wait for the commencement of the trial changed the mood of Machynlleth.

'We were all geared up for the trial in February,' recalls then town mayor Gareth Jones, 'but we had to put everything on hold for another two months. That was a strange limbo feeling, as if everything we had been gearing up for was taken away at the last minute.'

When the trial eventually did start, there was increased anxiousness in the town. 'A strange foreboding', one person called it, an anticipation of something of which they weren't sure. Since the Bridger arrest, most in the town believed that he was the person responsible for taking little April's life. The police case seemed credible. And this, despite the fact that everyone spoken to for this book said, without question, that Bridger had never given any indication, before October, that he was capable of the crimes he was charged with. But as the trial got underway, the town braced itself for what would be revealed.

'There was that feeling around that he hadn't actually been proven guilty,' says one mother from Bryn y Gog, 'and whatever we believed all along, there was still that outside slim chance that it might not all be true after all. It was probably an irrational way of thinking and didn't make much sense, but we did sort of hang on to the possibility.'

'We didn't actually talk a lot about that,' a friend of hers added, 'it wasn't the case that we sat around and chatted it all through, but we probably all thought it in the back of our minds. It was a kind of the elephant in the room all the time the trial was on.'

Susan Dale says that the services of Listening Point, especially the phone-in counselling, saw a dramatic increase as the trial approached and throughout the five weeks it lasted.

'Following our move, there was a change in the kind of people who called at the drop-in centre. They were understandably more from the estate itself from then on and that took on a new significance when the trial started. There was more of a need to keep in touch. And also during the time of the trial itself, the number of calls to the helpline went up to about eight a day. Those calls mainly came from the outlying villages surrounding Machynlleth town, and especially Ceinws itself where Mark Bridger lived.'

No doubt the people of Ceinws felt a dark shadow hanging over their village for the five weeks of the trial. If Machynlleth had to live with the knowledge that it was one of their own who was facing such evil charges, Ceinws knew that that same person lived in their village and that it was likely that the atrocities had been committed in the house down the road.

The description of Bridger throughout the trial particularly annoyed and angered many people. John Rogers sums it up:

'Everybody called him a local man – that really does bug me. He is not a local man. Yes, he's lived here for 20 years and yes he has children here who go to the local school. We had accepted him into the community. But he's not a local man, no way. That might seem a little point, but it's not to us, no way.'

There was a need to know what was going on, a need to know that they weren't on their own, a need to talk and offload, a need to keep in touch with others going through the same thing, a need to try and deal with the 'what in the earth do we do?' feelings that were taking over. For many, it was the shortest question of all that they tried to get the answer to as the detailed catalogue of horror unfolded in Mold Crown Court – why?

The trial wasn't able to give a satisfactory answer to the bigger questions this atrocity raised. Not only the 'why?' wasn't answered, but too many of the 'what happened?' questions weren't answered either. The family went though nothing short of hell in Mold. Paul and Coral were there every day listening to gory and gruesome details of what was probably done to their daughter. But after countless days of argument and counter-argument, with witness and expert testimony, they still didn't know the whereabouts of their daughter's body. It must have been agony for them to walk away from that court at the end of May having heard what Bridger probably did to their daughter but still not know where her final resting place was. One sentence from Bridger would have put an end to what turned out to be the longest police search in British police history and, more importantly, would have spared Paul and Coral and the rest of April's family, five weeks of trial hell in having to listen to him repeating stories that were an obvious fabrication and, as such, masked the truth of what really happened to their daughter. Above all else, it deprived them of the knowledge that might have led them to where she had been put by him; it deprived them of knowing where her final resting place was.

At the end of proceedings in the Crown Court, Coral's Victim Impact Statement was read out. It made upsetting reading:

> I am Coral Joyce Jones and I am the mother of April Sue Lyn Jones.
>
> In addition to previous statements I have made I also wish to make a statement in relation to the devastating effect the loss of our beautiful daughter April has had on me and my family.
>
> Words alone cannot describe how we are feeling or how we manage to function on a daily basis and I would never ever want any other family to go through what we are and will go through for the rest of our lives.

April was born prematurely, weighing only 4lbs 2oz, and was in intensive care for two weeks.

She has always been a little fighter and we later found out that she had a hole in her heart and a heart murmur.

When she was around three years old we noticed that she was becoming clumsy, so after numerous visits to the doctors they finally diagnosed April with cerebral palsy down her left side from her hip to her leg.

She became a guinea pig for other children, in that she was measured for a special suit to support her growing bones and if this suit was successful they would make suits for other children.

We would have to massage her legs and get her to do exercises because she would have pain in her legs constantly. She very rarely moaned about the pain and would be always on the go, wanting to go out to play with her friends.

April ruled our lives. She was the youngest and because of her various disabilities we would have to provide some kind of care for her all the time.

Paul would get her ready for school and then I would be there when she came home. I still cannot go into her bedroom to sort out her clothes, because the pain of her not being there is indescribable.

I have to watch [sister] and [brother] grieve for the loss of their little sister, whom they would carry upstairs because sometimes she was in too much pain to walk.

I have to see people whom I have known for years cross the road to avoid me because they do not know what to say to me.

At Christmas I tried to make it as normal as possible but would find myself breaking down in tears when I would be in a shop and I would see April's favourite "Little Kitty" things and anything pink, which was her favourite colour.

I broke my heart whilst writing Christmas cards and wondered whether I should put April's name on the cards. In the end I decided to just put a pink bow instead of April's name as a symbol of hope for our lovely girl.

I will never forget the night of 1 October 2012. This was the night that we allowed our daughter April to go out to play with her friends, something she has done hundreds of times before, and this is the night that she never came home.

Since that night, the estate is quiet, as the children are no longer allowed to go out to play as they used to.

As April's mother I will live with the guilt of letting her go out to play on the estate that night for the rest of my life.

She fought to come into the world, she fought to stay in this world, and he has taken her not only from us, but from everyone who loved her.

I will never see her smile again or hear her stomping around upstairs and on to the landing.

We will never see her bring home her first boyfriend and Paul will never walk her down the aisle.

How will we ever get over it?

No-one can answer Coral's question. People can support, offer practical help, say they're there if needed. They can pray if that's what they do. But no-one can get into the tortured minds and souls of Paul, Coral and their other children and sort things out for them so that they can 'get over it'.

The town and the area found the weeks of the trial particularly difficult. Kathleen Rogers describes the atmosphere during those weeks quite graphically.

'It was very edgy in town, it was awful. As the facts were being revealed in court, it certainly affected us and you could feel it on the streets. The town just collapsed on itself again. It was horrendous, horrendous. On the last two days of the trial it got worse in town. It was awful. Dark and quiet with no-one talking much to each other. We all felt a cloud over us, we all felt it at the same time without having to talk about it. We were all waiting for the same news but we all didn't want to hear it either.'

That feeling took on a new twist again when the jury returned to the courtroom with their verdict. The forewoman of the jury stood and stared straight at Bridger as she delivered their guilty verdict. He stood in the dock with his head tilted back and his eyes closed. Some suggested that was to hold back tears. There was nothing in the way he had reacted since his arrest that suggested that he was capable of such remorseful human emotion.

The guilty verdict in itself had a definite impact on the people in whose midst Mark Bridger had lived until a few months before. The people he drank with, played darts with, shopped with, went hunting with, the teachers at his children's schools and his neighbours in Ceinws, his ex-partners and their families all now knew, beyond any reasonable doubt, that he was the one who had taken and killed April.

The trial judge, Mr Justice John Griffith Williams, summing up, gave a clear view of what kind of man he thought Bridger was:

> There is no doubt in my mind that you are a paedophile who has for some time harboured sexual and morbid fantasies about young girls, storing on your laptop not only images of prepubescent and pubescent girls, but foul pornography of the gross sexual abuse of young children.
>
> What prompted you to live out one of those fantasies is a matter for speculation but it may have been the combination of the ending of one sexual relationship and your drinking. Whatever, you set out to find a little girl to abuse. I am not sure you targeted April specifically – it was probably fortuitous that she can be seen on some of the images, which you stored on your laptop, of her older sister – but you were on the prowl for a young girl.

On the streets of Machynlleth, there was stunned silence as this news filtered out. On the afternoon of Thursday, 30 May 2013, another event contributed to the way the town felt. Kathleen Rogers conducted the funeral a very popular man from the town who had suddenly passed away. His funeral at St Peter's was large, with the church full to the brim.

'I was walking to the church ready to conduct this funeral service. I stopped by the bank to get money from the cash point, when I had a text from the court with just one word in it. Guilty. I looked around me at the others on the streets of Mach and it was as if the whole town stopped. It was really strange.'

Kathleen Rogers had no more time to take in the news she's just had or to discuss it with anyone. She was off to the church.

In one of the businesses not far from that bank, one mother was at work when the news came through:

'I was sick three times on hearing the news that Bridger was guilty. My stomach couldn't take the fact that he had actually done all those things we had heard over the months and especially during the trial. We had kept a close eye on how things were going in the trial. We wanted to know what was going on even though in a way we didn't want to know too. So we knew the facts. The verdict was the realisation that it actually was as we had heard. Hearing the judge say that he thought Bridger was a paedophile was as sickening as anything. We just sat around in work wondering out loud to each other in disjointed sentences, what must he have done to that poor girl? We knew him as a father, we saw him in school, his kids played with our children... I just can't think about that, even now.'

'I had always thought,' a worker in another Machynlleth shop said, 'that as long as he goes down, it will be OK. My wife and I had kept in touch with how things were going as I think everybody here did. We heard or read what he had done and if the word guilty comes through then that's what should happen and that will be the end of it. But it didn't happen that way. There was no sense of ending, bringing things to a close and neither was there any rejoicing.'

Many were struck by the fact that it was 'one of their own' who was now formally guilty of such horrendous acts, with many seeing the broader relevance.

'People talk about this thing called "stranger danger",' a hospital worker commented in one of the town's cafés. 'But this shows clearly that that whole idea might be way off the mark. It doesn't seem to me that such a thing is the issue really, especially if you look at what happened in Soham as well. Huntley and Carr knew the two little girls who were taken and killed, and there are so many other similar stories. It hasn't made us wary of strangers at least in Mach, there's no point because that just doesn't add up to the facts.'

On verdict day, the few who were on the town's streets weren't saying much to each other, in contrast to before when every conversation turned to April's story in an attempt to stay together and bond their hope. That day it was a nod in passing. Everyone knew what everyone else was feeling and a gestured acknowledgement of that was more than enough.

Alyson Jones turned up to work at Losin Lush as usual that day. But it didn't last.

'I felt awful, like everyone else. The mood in the town was not nice at all. It was as if there was a cloak thrown over us. Very few people were out on the streets. I decided to close the shop for the day. Staying open wasn't important at all at that point, so I went home.'

The whole story had another effect on Alyson too. Details of Bridger's actions, as well as the judge's comments, made her think of the whole incident in a way others hadn't.

'What stories like this do is to bring things back to people who might have been through something traumatic in their own past. That was certainly true in my case. I was abused when I was a young girl, on more than one occasion by two different men. I have been very fortunate to be able to deal with that over the years and move on from the trauma. But there's no doubt that hearing the details of this story, of something having happened to a little girl in my town who I knew, and by a man from this town I was familiar with, it brought things back again for me. It was a very uncomfortable time, distressing at some times too, as everything became so real and close to me.

'To a lesser extent, I felt the same before Christmas when the search was still very much on. In light of what was happening in Mach and what we feared then might have happened to April, it was impossible for me to watch the drama series *Broadchurch*. I know that others in the town who have not been through what I have, also reacted in the same way. That was really unfortunate timing and no-one could have foreseen that, but it did affect us.

'But I do think that the kind of reaction I went through because of this story should be something that the media should consider in the reporting of such stories too. It's right that the deeds of perpetrators of this kind are exposed. But there must be some consideration for how that reporting affects victims too. I'm lucky, I can talk about it, but not everyone can.'

The comment about *Broadchurch* echoes a similar point made by Kevin Wells in relation to the disappearance of his daughter, Jessica. A popular TV drama, at the time of that incident, also dealt with a topic painfully close to the reality the Wells and Chapman families were experiencing.

Kevin Wells said that a policeman: '... warns me that tonight's episode of *A Touch of Frost* is about a paedophile kidnapping. "I thought I'd better let you know, just in case, well you know..." I stop him mid-sentence to thank him. We will not be tuning in.'

By three o'clock that afternoon, Kathleen Rogers had completed her duties at the funeral and had made her way from the church to the town centre. She had told the media beforehand that she would not be able to give her reaction if the verdict came through during the funeral. It did arrive then, and she knew that there would be a barrage of media crews and reporters waiting for her when she was free.

'There were over 50 messages on my mobile by the time I left the church. I stood in the town, on one side of one street or the other from about three o'clock until gone eight that evening, answering all sorts of questions from all sorts of news sources. They had to tell me what the sentence was as I didn't know that before going to the funeral service.

'There was nobody about by then, nobody. You would think, wouldn't you, that people would be dancing in the streets or something, showing their relief that justice had been done, showing a sense of vindication? But no, there was none of that. Nothing.'

Others reacted throughout the UK, of course, and one of those involved in the search on that first day, was working in the north of England on the railways when the verdict came through. John Rogers was in Carnforth at the time.

'I was sat in the bar of the hotel in which I was staying, with a gang of other railwaymen when the news came on the television. I was hearing the verdict and seeing the streets of my home town in a bar in a faraway place. It was strange to say the least; it was weird and it was horrible and I'm not overusing those words. But, at the same time, with all those people around me, it also felt as if I was "home" in another way, because everyone could identify with April's story. One person, in particular, had kept in touch with me since the very first day of the story. He was an ex-policeman, from Carnforth, and he'd been texting me regularly, daily at one point, asking if we needed this, that or the other, to help us in our search. I was sat with him when the verdict came through. So there was a lot of empathy with what we had been through and that was a help to me, being so far away from Mach when the verdict came through.'

If the people of Machynlleth and the Dyfi Valley were absent from the streets on verdict day, the streets were busy enough with television, radio and newspaper people. They dominated the town, as they had done on many other occasions since October. Of all the comments given in relation to this book, there is only one comment that has been consistently heard from every single person talked to: harsh criticism of the way that the town and its people were treated by the media. Initially, the support and cooperation that the various news programmes and publications gave the people of Machynlleth was warmly welcomed. But, Gareth Jones, for example, then noticed a change in that relationship.

'For the first few days of the search, there was an easy relationship between us and all the crews and reporters who descended on the town. We had the information they wanted about April and the search for her and we realised that we

147

needed to get the message out as fast as we could, so the news programmes were essential for us too. People wanted to know what was going on and the news was the way of finding out. But, as soon as Bridger was charged with murder, things changed. They didn't want to know about us then, the people of the town, they wanted to know everything about him, all the background details they could get. I noticed this because I was interviewed regularly during those early days and then the questions I was being asked changed and I was being asked about one man only. There was no interest in what was going on amongst the same group of people who had been of massive interest to them initially, even though that story was also developing.'

Others in the town, and on the Bryn y Gog estate specifically, tell similar stories. One worker in an eating place in the town said that one crew, in particular, would come in, in a fairly large group, and sit round the table discussing details of either the search, investigation or the trial and their coverage of it, with everyone else having to hear everything.

'I had to ask them in the end not to be so insensitive to the needs of the others who might have been there for a family meal or a meal for two, or whatever. They didn't want to hear gory details of a murder trial.'

'On the estate,' the single mother we've heard from before says, 'we were afraid to walk across the paths back and forth between our own houses. We would regularly be approached by a reporter from a newspaper or have a camera shoved in our faces. I must say that it is a difficult point really, because I was one of those who turned to the news all day to see what was going on, so I realise I might be a bit of a hypocrite. But I think it's more the way they are so intrusive and in your face that really upset us and got our backs up too.'

It was the methods used to get stories that certainly annoyed a group of three men in the bar of the town's Wynnstay Hotel. They saw a practice they obviously disapproved of.

'It happened in our cafés more often than not,' one

explained, 'a group of people, two, three, four, or whatever, would be sitting having a chat when they would notice someone sitting on their own nearby with a little recorder pointing in their direction, recording what they were saying. The people weren't even asked if they minded. That kind of intrusion and arrogance we won't miss, we're glad to see the back of them!'

They also speak of being offered money in exchange for information – a practice they readily accept is quite common – but one they felt particularly unhappy with in the context of this story.

'I don't think any one of us would even dream of taking money for some information about April or her family. We don't work like that.'

Many interviews for this book were agreed only after assurances were received that the enquiry was not one for a newspaper. Some refused because they didn't want to speak to a journalist about April's story again, with authors and journalists, books and newspapers, being tarred by the same brush. Another, who was constantly, if reluctantly, in the media spotlight was often surprised at the type of questions she was asked.

'Being asked "How do they feel?" on leaving a particularly difficult public meeting wasn't exactly the brightest question I've been asked,' says Kathleen Rogers. 'But another question I was asked on the day of the verdict seems to have annoyed quite a few people in Mach. Within a couple of hours of hearing the news that Bridger was guilty, I was asked if we would be able to forgive him. I think the general consensus of those who saw the interview on TV was what a bloody stupid question to ask on that bloody day! We are, of course, all asked to forgive and I believe that. But not on the day we hear that it's confirmed that he actually did what we'd all feared all along. Forgiveness takes time.'

Author Mike Parker takes particular exception to the way the media portrayed the area, as well as agreeing with the comments made by others about the intrusive nature of their way of working.

'Bridger had only lived in Ceinws for about three or four weeks and the people there really didn't know him. But when journalists and reporters went door-knocking in the village to ask the neighbours, "What sort of man is he?" they didn't like the answer they got. They were told no, they didn't know anything about him. This was immediately taken as a small rural community closing ranks and refusing to cooperate. For the villagers, "no" was an honest answer, for the media, it was a suspicious one.'

This approach, according to Mike Parker, was indicative of a deeper attitude towards the area. He also takes particular exception to the way the area was described.

'They came here with a seemingly clear flat-packed idea of what such a rural Welsh community should be and just assembled it in the Dyfi Valley. I'm sure some thought they were coming to Trumpton where they would portray a countryside murder story to the world. One small example: they spoke of Bridger's home as a remote farmhouse. It is neither. It's a former slate manager's house in the middle of a village! These perceptions became part of the unfolding narrative. It's also, to a large extent, why there was a dislike of the way the media operated. We didn't like the way we were being described and what we saw on TV about Mach was different to the lives we led from day to day in the same town.'

A few weeks after the verdict, a TV satellite van turned up on the Bryn y Gog estate. The crew was there to interview Paul and Coral. Before it arrived, on a hot summer's day, there were many children out playing on the estate's large grassy areas. As soon as the van turned up, the children either went, or were called, indoors. It was a flashback to the past and an indication that they didn't want to return there again.

With the end of the trial and verdict, there was some sort of closure for the people of Machynlleth. But any suggestion that the end of that chapter was *actual* closure for those people is clearly refuted. One columnist, Cris Dafis, in Welsh magazine *Golwg*, said that as for the people of Machynlleth being able to have closure now the case was over, such a concept was the result of media use of an Americanism that actually didn't exist.

What lay before the people of the Dyfi Valley was not a sense that everything was now over, but a real sense that there was a new way of coping ahead of them, as uncertain and confused as any step they had previously been forced to take.

10

April's Law

As May turned to June, and eight months since April's disappearance turned into a ninth, a new chapter began for the people of Machynlleth and the Dyfi Valley. The perpetrator was behind bars and the reality that April would never be found was reluctantly being accepted. So, what would happen next?

The most obvious next milestone in the story would be the public outcry in relation to the downloading of images of children for pornographic purposes from the Internet. There was revulsion when it was revealed the kind of images Bridger had stored on his computer and had viewed on the day he took April. In a detailed article on the whole case, the *New Zealand Herald* sums up exactly what Bridger had stored, showing the degree of interest worldwide in this story:

'The disturbing cache included 65 criminal-standard abuse images. Carefully categorised into folders were pictures of Soham murder victims Holly Wells and Jessica Chapman and British schoolgirl Caroline Dickinson who was raped and killed on a school trip to France in 1996.

'The illegal pictures were kept away from holiday snaps in anonymous files, including one marked "Z0" that contained obscene imagery of child abuse.

'Another was marked "clothed" and the other bore the name of April's 16-year-old half-sister who he had described as "beautiful" and an "up and coming model". She had earlier refused a Facebook request to befriend the 47-year-old on the advice of her mother. Bridger set his own Facebook settings to maximum and concealed his age.'

The newspapers after the conclusion of the trial were in no doubt as to the cause and effect relationship between Bridger's viewings and his actions. Murder of April 'proves porn link to sex assaults' said the *Daily Telegraph*. The *Daily Mail* asked, 'What *will* it take for Google to block child porn?' The *Sun* devoted an editorial to the same issue and the *Mirror* included a comment column by Jon Brown, the head of the NSPCC programme which tackles sex abuse.

In that article, he says that in 1990 there were 7,000 hard copies of indecent images in England and Wales but a year ago just five police forces reported they had confiscated 26 million images from offenders. What happened in the intervening years was the Internet. He also says that a recent NSPCC study found that one in three men found guilty of possessing or downloading such images had also committed other sex crimes.

His message is clear: 'Action on internet child pornography is long overdue and we have reached the tipping point where something has to be done.'

April's parents are convinced that the images Bridger viewed the day he took their daughter were a significant factor in the actions he then took. The *Sun* turned that into a campaign called April's Law, echoing Sarah's Law, a similar campaign mounted following the disappearance of Sarah Payne. Sarah Payne was seven years old when she was taken and killed in 2000. The *News of the World* launched the campaign to lobby for parents' right to know if there was someone registered on the sex offenders' register living in their area. It turned out that the man convicted of Sarah's murder, Roy Whiting, was on that register and lived not far from Sarah and her family. The campaign was based on an American example, Megan's Law, which was set up after Megan Kanka was raped and murdered by her neighbour in 1994. After the killer's trial, it was revealed that he was a convicted child rapist. Megan's Law has resulted in photographs and addresses of sex offenders being available. Sarah's Law gives fewer details.

Paul and Coral met Sarah Payne's mother, Sara, to see how a campaign in the name of their daughter could learn from the previous one. Sara Payne and her son are to help Paul and Coral set up a website to further their aim of pushing for limits to the kind of child-related pornographic images which are able to be downloaded from the Internet. They have called for a warning system to be introduced which alerts Internet providers if indecent images of children are downloaded.

They made their intentions known on the *This Morning* TV programme, and the *Sun* newspaper has supported the campaign too. Sara Payne contributes a column to that paper. Under the heading 'Join our action to stop net perverts', Coral and Sara called on providers, such as Google, to clamp down on paedophiles.

Then, in mid July, Paul and Coral met Prime Minister David Cameron to argue the same case. Their meeting was held ahead of a prearranged one between the Prime Minister and providers such as Google and BT to discuss wider issues. The Joneses were joined in Downing Street by the parents of murdered twelve-year-old Tia Sharp, who died at the hands of a man who had viewed indecent images the day she disappeared. Following that meeting, the Prime Minister announced that he was planning to introduce automatic web filters unless customers opted out. He also said he would introduce legislation to create a new offence of possession of pornography simulating rape, as well as new powers for watchdogs to access heavily encrypted sites, and he vowed to urge search engines to ban searches for child abuse. Google have since confirmed that their engineers are working on a system that will filter such images. In discussing this point however, leading Welsh journalist Carolyn Hitt said this in her column on *Wales Online*:

'But this is a reactive rather than a proactive approach. As John Carr, a Government adviser and member of the Internet Task Force on Child Protection, explains, Google have a Safe Search facility which blocks child pornography. If they made this their default search facility, those who wanted to trawl the Internet for vile images would have to register, making themselves visible. At present they can remain anonymous – until, that is, the police discover the content of their computers in the devastating aftermath of a case of child abuse or even murder.

'It is too late to respond to online paedophilia in the reactive way Google currently advocates. They – and every Internet search engine provider – must show moral leadership. "Google are the biggest players," Mr Carr told the BBC's *Today* programme. "If they were to block it, others would follow."

'If the pictures of April's smiling face continue to resonate, the words her mother spoke so bravely in her victim impact statement will stay with us too. Describing April's premature birth and the challenge of the disabilities she faced, Coral Jones said: "April fought to come into the world, she fought to stay in this world, and he has taken her, not only from us, but from everyone who loved her."

'These words are simply heart-breaking but one way of honouring the memory of April Jones would be for every one of us to channel her fighting spirit and battle the internet giants to block the evils of child porn.'

A major recent contribution was made to this debate by the release of a groundbreaking film. Award-winning director, Beeban Kidron, who made the classic *Oranges Are Not the Only Fruit* film in 1989, has made a film called *InRealLife* which looks at the way technology such as smartphones and the Internet affect the lives of teenagers in Britain today. In an *Observer* article to coincide with the launch of the film, she calls for a change of culture to respond to the growing Internet influence, not just legislation. A change of culture she says, such has happened in our attitudes to smoking. But most of the responsibility she believes lies with the corporations:

'I think it is up to the providers of any service to deliver safe goods and we need to let them know that. The idea that these people cannot put their resources to uncover the source of child pornography, or cannot work out the ways to pursue bullies who send death and rape threats is patently absurd. They can afford it and we should demand it of them.'

Overwhelming public sentiment is right behind such thoughts. Many believe that the gestures made so far, in the name of April's Law, by the media or government, fall far short of anything credible and workable and they would prove to be no deterrent to anyone who wanted to continue to view such images. Others argue that this is a restriction of human rights. These arguments will no doubt go on and on, but so does the April's Law campaign.

The end of the trial saw Paul and Coral speak for the first time on the television about their ordeal. They used the opportunity mostly to promote April's Law. But they did also talk about some aspects of what they had been through since the day April disappeared. They joined in the search of the surrounding roads and streets, and they revealed after the trial that they were just one-and-a-half miles behind April, with Coral expressing the heartfelt question that will haunt her forever, 'If only we knew what vehicle we were looking for...'

They said that they were kept well informed by the police of every new development in the investigation and that hearing that April's blood was found in Bridger's home was the worst part of it all for them. Paul Jones said:

'The hard part about it is that, because we had so much evidence and the police had kept us so well up-to-date, we have a good idea what happened – and then he's just spinning lies to fit the situation. It was hard to listen to that because he was talking about April, how he tried to help her, how she was crushed and he couldn't remember what he had done with her. It sends shivers up your back.'

One particular comment made by Bridger repeatedly during the trial upset both parents every time it was said. 'He was calling her "little April". He had no right to call her "little April".'

Her parents said that they will never seek to ask Bridger

what he did with their daughter, because, as Coral put it, that would put him in control again.

During the trial, one group associated with the story from the outset, and who had received praise, were beginning to be questioned. Originally, the police had received nothing but admiration and support. But, questions were now being asked, especially by people in Ceinws. Many raised concerns as to the way their village was dug up time and time again. It had, said one, made them 'very jumpy'.

'We couldn't stand the bright arc lights blazing through our windows at night,' says one elderly man from the village, 'it was impossible to sleep. Some live here on their own and it was a very frightening place to be. Did they have to be here at night to do that?'

In Machynlleth, similar questions were asked. 'If they have so much forensic evidence why is their search so extensive?' one man asks in a café. 'It doesn't make sense.'

His colleague offers a possible explanation. 'It all sounds like a massive PR job for the police to me. Why do they launch the largest police search in British history at a time there's a real threat to police budgets? There must be a link.'

The questioning all relates to the way the police treated people and the scale of the operation. With regards to the latter point, particular comment was made about the fact that, with so many officers being brought in from other areas, a briefing session had to be held every time a new group arrived.

'That must have led to a lot of repetition. Is that why so many gardens were dug up three, four, five times?'

Whatever the accuracy of the comments made, the relevant point is that questions were being asked. It would have been unthinkable for anyone to say anything of the sort in public as recently as the beginning of the trial. It was just one sign that attitudes were changing.

11

A fragile hope

As APRIL'S PARENTS began to make more public comments, and the world got glimpses of the harrowing time they had endured, Machynlleth was also coming to terms with the way it would move forward. Those who visited the area in order to report on the tragedy, or to be involved in some other aspect of the story, soon commented on the spirit and the resolve they saw among the people of the Dyfi Valley. After the service on that first Sunday, the Bishop of Bangor, the Right Reverend Andrew John said:

'There's a real strength to this community, but I've also been struck by how people have refused to allow this terrible incident to become a commentary on Machynlleth. There's almost a defiance in the way they're acting – Machynlleth isn't like this; we're better than this.'

The reputation of being a safe place is something that has been consistently repeated about Machynlleth. The press used the word many times in reporting April's story. Some saw this 'safeness' as now being shaken or damaged, including one MP, Glyn Davies: 'The fact that the evil shadow descended in the midst of a place like this, one of the safest in the Britain, has made people realise it could happen anywhere and that's why it has had such a huge impact.'

Susan Lee, in the *Liverpool Echo*, was particularly struck by what she saw in the town:

'But while we shake our heads in sorrowful disbelief there is comfort, albeit small, to be drawn from this terrible episode and it is this: there is more good in the world than bad. Machynlleth has proved it. For while the town will always carry the weight of the events of recent days and the stain of potentially the very worst of human nature, it has also shown us the very best.

'Machynlleth was and is a town united. Sometimes, reading the papers or watching the news, it is easy to believe we are a selfish society, looking out only for number one; a country where we all live isolated from each other. But that's not true. Random acts of kindness take place every day; neighbours go out of their way to help each other for no reward. And when a mum and dad are in the most desperate need of their lives, their pleas will be answered by people they've never even met.

'In the darkness of the days that stretched into weeks and months, the only light came from the compassion of those who never gave up hope April would be found. The people of Machynlleth became one family, drawing the little girl's relatives into their embrace and showing the outside world a united front through the symbolism of the pink ribbon. It was an inspirational and deeply moving demonstration of the power of community.'

Carolyn Hitt, in conversation with the author as a year is marked since April's disappearance, looks back at the way the community responded with one clear thought in mind.

'It's about the choice that the people of that area clearly made, even if it wasn't of necessity a conscious one; they chose to show the innocence and good side of human nature as opposed to dwelling on the evil that was so obviously done right in their midst.

'The most unimaginable evil and trauma and the worst possible experience a family can have is what April's family experienced, but the reaction to that showed that there was a bigger family who wanted to look after them.

'That sense of community I would like to think is unique to a Welsh environment and the impact of what happened is made all the more difficult to take in by the fact that it was someone, not only from that community, but from such a community, who committed the most horrible acts against a child also from that community. The uniqueness of the response shook me at the time and I think that people went to Machynlleth from outside the area because they saw how special that community was.

'The local people there were obviously keen to show that they weren't about shouting and screaming in anger, rage or bitterness. They rose above that. They wanted to focus everything on April, on the little girl, on her innocence and not his evil. That was the only thing they could cling to through everything. A crime like this shatters all that humanity is about and I think people wanted to prove their humanity in a more positive way.'

Another analysis came from renowned author and *Guardian* columnist, George Monbiot, who lives in Machynlleth. His headline for the piece he wrote for the *Guardian* the day after the verdict captures his thoughts: 'April's murder tested the strength of my community'. He says that he wrote an article three years ago advocating the development of housing estates which were safe areas of housing because of the way they had been designed. A central feature of such sites was that the houses faced inwards and children could play safely in full view of their carers. He gave an example of such an estate, the one across the road from where he lived, Bryn y Gog. This tragedy rocked that assumption and he goes on to say:

'Until now I have not been able to write about it or speak about it. After the reports of the first day of Mark Bridger's trial, I have been unable to read about it either. I've long prided myself on being able to handle more reality than most, but with this case I've discovered my limits. For everyone connected with Machynlleth, the experience has been shattering. It has shattered our sense of contingency, broken the boundaries of what we considered reality. In his novel *The Sleep of Reason*, about a similarly hideous case, C P Snow wrote of "the hallucinations of fact". I now know what he meant.'

Having been brutally honest about the thoughts that had gone through his mind about what he'd like to do with Bridger, he says that such vindictive considerations are now gone: 'Though April is lost for ever, the awful wounds her abduction and killing have inflicted on Machynlleth will begin, very slowly, to heal.

'Already a sense of resilience and defiance is growing in the town. People are slowly emerging from the carapace of shock. And from the green on the estate comes the most beautiful sound on earth, the sound of healing: children playing. Their happy voices, ringing out once more, are the best memorial that little girl could have.'

Machynlleth itself now needs to know how it is going to cope. As the schools broke up for the summer, there was a change in the mood of the town and its people. There was a united desire to find ways of moving on – but not so much unity in the ways they could do so. For the first time the people of Machynlleth were not as one.

On that first day of October they'd been thrown together, united in hope, confusion, darkness, horror, revulsion. They searched as one, they created support networks for police, emergency and rescue services as one team, they raised money as one, and they dealt with questions and answers as one. They came together on that Sunday, on the streets and in the pews, as one. The shroud of darkness and silence held them in its grip as one during the five-week trial.

They walked united into the unfolding drama of the murder of one of the town's children. But less than a year later, they were walking out of it, out of step. Grief was becoming more personal than public, more individual than mass. Their joined-up compassion is now showing its fragmented aftermath. This is not to suggest that any element of antagonism, falling out or any other negative association is now becoming evident. Different ways of dealing with the same situation are now becoming more evident.

The way people attached themselves to this story seems

to now have a bearing on the way they are trying to move forward. At the centre of the events was obviously the Bryn y Gog estate. April's taking happened in their midst. The people of the town were caught up in that event. The people of Ceinws were thrown into events in a different way again. This is not to suggest that there are degrees of grief, that some have been harder hit than others just because of where they live. No-one who is a part of this story is more peripheral just because of the geography of their involvement, no-one's feelings more marginalised because of their postcode. But the emotional and psychological impact was, of course, far greater on those in the closest vicinity as opposed to those from much further afield. People on the outside looking in were indeed looking through a glass darkly, but they could, and did, still 'feel'.

There is an increasing difference in the way that the people at the epicentre of this tragedy are now talking about the way they have been affected.

'I've certainly heard more and more people saying that they feel angry and bitter towards Bridger,' says Gareth Jones, 'That wasn't obvious at all for months and months but now it's a little more open. Parents tell me that their children are more outwardly disturbed now that the school holidays are here. It's all relative, in that it isn't at epidemic proportions, but it's more than there has been to date in Mach.'

One feature of the way the area initially reacted was that distinct lack of anger and bitterness. There have been no public displays of outrage or anger at all. During the trial, for example, a banner calling for Bridger to be dealt with severely was draped on the town clock. It was immediately taken down. John Rogers sums up this by noting:

'The one thing I said from day one was not to publicly show any anger because that would make us look bad then. If we showed restraint and respect, we would show that we are better than the chap who did what he did. If we would have started to throw eggs at vans and shouted and bawled in the court, then all the good that the community have done together is tarred.

We can all talk about how we feel over a pint in the pub; we can say what we feel and what we would like to see done to Bridger. But it stays there. We don't bring it out into the public. What we actually did was to channel any anger into all the things we did together as a community, frustrations have been channelled into sorting out what needed to be sorted out.'

The townspeople are also more than aware that Bridger has children who still live there. The public restraint is then needed to protect them as well.

There are three visual symbols to show how the town is coping. At Bryn y Gog, there's the high-profile garden which is impossible to miss. It's the most prominent memorial to a little girl's killing, yards from where she lived, the most obvious physical feature linked to the murder, right where the drama started. It is, as one resident put it, 'in your face'. There was a sense of discomfort in uttering those words, because now some are beginning to question whether the garden is needed any longer. Some say it's time for it to go. One parent said that she now walked the long way in and out of the estate in order to avoid seeing it. It's a constant reminder, said another, of what we want to forget.

A man who works in the town said that he regularly walked up past Bryn y Gog to the hills. Now he doesn't because he doesn't want to see the garden. Not one person who shared these thoughts harboured any iota of ill-feeling towards Coral and Paul and the family. It isn't about that. It's about coping. It's about dealing with feelings. The most dramatic memorial then, the one that poses the biggest dilemma, is right where April was taken.

Others take a completely different view. They say it's far too soon to talk of dismantling the garden; the memory, the feelings are still raw and it's a fitting tribute to what April herself, her family and the townspeople went through. A young woman from the estate said that it was not up to them to say when anything should be moved or taken down. That was up to Coral and Paul, she said. It is, quite simply, their tragedy and their tragedy alone.

'Find April Jones' Facebook page administrator, Beckah Pughe, agrees:

'How can we know when is the right time to stop grieving? It's not our tragedy, we haven't lost a five-year-old daughter, Paul and Coral have, so they know when they don't want to see the garden anymore, they know when the ribbons need to come down. All we can do is stand with them until such a time as they are ready.'

When the same argument is applied to the ribbons that are still to be seen around the town, the feelings are very similar. It's time to take them down now, say some, while others say that it's still necessary to put up new ones if the present ones are frayed. The ones who advocate keeping things as they are speak far more dogmatically than those who think it's time for change. 'We will never take the ribbons down' is the language used by those for the status quo, while those who want change merely suggest, quietly and in apologetic tones, that is what should happen. They certainly don't want to put their names to such comments. They are more than aware that they don't want their opinions to be interpreted as being callous, hard-hearted and as criticisms of Paul and Coral.

The second symbol is the Hugging Tree. It overlooks the town centre, high on a hill, tucked away in a clearing amidst other trees. A person needs to choose whether to go to see this memorial. It's a contemplative place and a visit there is like a visit to a church. You decide to go there when you need to, for the reason you need to go there. It's a deliberate mourning, a spiritual act.

And then there's the third visual symbol, a white cottage in a small village. This cottage is overlooked more than any other in the entire settlement, right by the side of the main road, seen by all who live there and drive through. The residents have no choice but to see it. It now stands empty, a haunting shell of dark secrets, and a macabre memorial to the place where April probably breathed her last breath. No bright pinks and blues here as in the Bryn y Gog garden and the Hugging Tree. No plants or growth to signify new life and new beginnings. No artefacts painted bright and cheerful by children to lift the gloom. It stands for the horror that no-one can avoid. Little wonder then that Paul and Coral have called for it to be demolished completely. This is also some sort of shrine for those who think that there is no light in this story, those who can't see that there is a way back. Maybe a poem written at the end of the troubles in Belfast makes this particular point clearly:

Progress

They say that for years Belfast was backwards
and it's great now to see some progress.
So I guess we can look forward to taking boxes
from the earth. I guess that ambulances
will leave the dying back amidst the rubble
to be explosively healed. Given time,
one hundred thousand particles of glass
will create impossible patterns in the air
before coalescing into the clarity
of a window. Through which, a reassembled head
will look out and admire the shy young man
taking his bomb from the building and driving home.

Allan Gillis

There won't ever be that sort of progress of course. But hopelessness isn't the only way for a broken community to react.

Three places. Three ways of grieving. As the months move on, the garden gives way to the tree and the cottage is gaining increasing attention. Gestures of hope and remembrance fade as acts of contemplation and outbursts of anger and bitterness take over. But through all this, there is attempt at living the normal Machynlleth life, of restoring its natural rhythm.

There have been many events in the area over the last few months which have been held as they normally would have but, this year, with the added intention of 'keeping things normal': the carnival, a fun day on Bryn y Gog and, of all things, a comedy festival.

Machynlleth had hosted a comedy festival in previous years. This year's event, already planned before October 2012, was due to happen on what turned out to be the first week of Bridger's trial. When this timing became evident, the organisers immediately contacted the town council to seek advice. The council decided that the event should go ahead, the town needed laughter, and it needed lifting. It wasn't considered to be inappropriate.

The carnival brought the people of the Dyfi Valley together for a reason that was not heavy with the significance of the loss of April. The service on the Sunday after her disappearance was only for her. The Christmas carol service by the clock had April's haunting pink shadow all over it. Other community events were held, such as a football match arranged by the Welsh Football Association, to raise money for the April Fund. The carnival went ahead in its usual format and many said that it had been a great help for the town to get together.

The team behind the Listening Point drop-in centre organised a fun day on the Bryn y Gog estate, predominantly for the sake of the children. Susan Dale sums the day up in this way:

'Listening Point was buzzing with volunteers – tins of hot dog sausages, bread rolls, gingerbread people for decorating and craft supplies. It felt daunting, way out of our comfort zone – how could we cook 750 hot dog sausages with a Baby Belling and an urn? It was really good to be part of something so positive happening on the estate, seeing people working together to make this happen. As the rain clouds lifted and things got underway, it was so good to see the children laughing and playing; it felt like a real step on the road to recovering normality.

'Just occasionally there were reminders of the trauma of the past months; the slight hesitation about "being photographed", the family who had travelled from Swindon to be with us, the pinkness of a child's teddy bear clutched under an arm, a few tears in the drop-in centre, but there was something about the "working together" to make it happen, and the event itself, which was such fun for the children that seemed to reconnect us all in different ways. It was as if the emphasis had changed from all of us being powerless in how we responded to these awful events, to being empowered and proactive in creating something positive for the children.'

There is indeed an all-round sense of creating something positive, for all the differences in opinions as to how exactly they do so. But in looking forward, the people of Machynlleth are also looking back. In its own way that is also part of moving ahead. There's a need to see what they have been able to glean from all the suffering they have been through, a need to find some silver linings somewhere among the black clouds. They have not been difficult to find.

Gareth Jones senses that the town has united in a way it hadn't before, not just for the most intense period of searching for April.

'Mach has always had three strands in the make-up of the town and the area, three types of people, if you like, who live here. There are the indigenous Welsh, who have the Dyfi Valley soil in their blood, there are those who've moved here from various parts of Wales and England, and there are those drawn here by the alternative way of living that the Centre for Alternative Technology stands for. We have carried on with our lives side-by-side quite happily, but never one group having much to do with the other. That has changed. There are obvious signs now of a blurring of those definition boundaries. I don't want to overstate the case, but it would be equally wrong to say it isn't happening. That is a good sign for Mach from now on.'

John Rogers agrees with Gareth Jones and is quite surprised as to how some people get on:

'During those first days of searching, I was driving a group of people around in a van and I remember looking round thinking that I couldn't believe that I had so-and-so and so-and-so in the same van with me! They hated each other normally, but there they were side-by-side. I've spoken to people I've fallen out with during the last months and it's still strange to look across the street sometimes and see who's with who. Don't get me wrong, they're not best mates or anything, but what I see now I would never have thought I would see.'

Machynlleth is like most other towns in one sense, because it too is suffering from economic decline. Shops stay empty and there's been a sharp rise in poverty there. According to an article in *Planet: The Welsh Internationalist* magazine in the summer of 2013, it is estimated that more than half the population of the town lives in fuel poverty. Again, such facts play into the way people responded. They are not wealthy, but they have shown a rich generosity of spirit. On a business level, shop owner Alyson Jones sees a legacy from the tragedy:

'There are many empty shops and we are obviously concerned as shop owners about this and the effect it has on the town. What has happened in the last few months is that a few of us have come together to discuss what we can do ourselves about it. I'm not too sure that would have happened before. It's as if we now see the benefit of cooperation, having pulled together for the best part of a year on such a deeply emotive issue.'

Some point to other differences in the town's life. Many mentioned that they had got to know their own locality far better as a result of being out searching. As one said:

'We have been so used to just jumping in the car to go from here to there, especially in my case as I work in Aberystwyth, so I just commute from here to there. Now I know areas within a square mile of where I live that I'd never been to before. I certainly appreciate my square mile more now.'

In the bar of the Wynnstay Hotel, two men say that Machynlleth is now a place in its own right. Previously, they said, they always told people that they lived just north of Aberystwyth as no-one actually knew the town in which they lived. Now they say they're from Machynlleth and even though people only know of the town because of a dark story, they take a great sense of identity in being able to name their own town.

Small, day-to-day steps on the road to healing the wounds. Added to that is the fact that what has been called the 'naughty element' of the town, has been really quiet for twelve months.

'We've had no trouble,' says Gareth Jones, 'with petty offences such as broken windows, graffiti, rowdy behaviour on weekends in the pubs. It's as if those who usually fall into that kind of thing have decided not to, that it isn't important any more. I don't think it will last, but it is quite encouraging that it has been on hold during this time.'

As far as episodes specific to April's story are concerned, there is one central event prominent by its absence. There has been no funeral for April. It's not been possible to conduct one because her body has not been found. But, this situation changed when bone fragments were found. There was now hope for a funeral service. As this book goes to print, there are plans for a service at St Peter's Church in Machynlleth. A horse and carriage will carry a pink coffin containing the bone fragments through the town. Maybe this will be another step in the recovery process.

The town is a different place since the taking of April and a lot of that is, ironically, for the good. There's a more positive change in the sense of identity, but some fear a stigma that Machynlleth will be another name on the list of towns associated with tragedy and evil acts. When Andy Murray, who comes from Dunblane, won Wimbledon this year, comment was made that his victory would help the town be remembered for something other than the tragedy there. The talk was of beginning to erase the stigma. That tragedy occurred in 1996.

But not many fear such a stigma in Machynlleth. One commented that that would not be the case because the English media can't pronounce Machynlleth anyway, so there was no danger of the town's name sticking to the story. It was more likely to carry April's own name.

The few words that Paul and Coral were prepared to say officially for this book, not surprisingly, were about the response of their own community from that first day of October. Paul sums up their feelings:

'For the first few days, we were caught up in the grief and sheer horror of having our daughter go missing. We could see the response on the grassy area outside our own home, there were hundreds of people there, but we couldn't really take it in. After a while, though, it started to sink in, the response and support of our neighbours started to dawn on us. It truly was amazing. It was so humbling to see people give up their time in order to help look for our daughter. If I could walk around this whole area personally pinning medals on the chest of every single person who helped in whichever way, then I would do it today.'

In July, as I sat with them in the back garden where April would have played and through which she left the house on that night, their son stood at the same gate asking to go out. His dad said yes and told him not to be long. The child went off into the community. The significance of his dad's words lay heavily in the air. But they were a sign that things had to be just so. They couldn't be any other way.

That same day, in the Wynnstay Hotel, an American mother was talking to her young son, no more than six years old. He wanted to go outside and asked if it was OK. His mum turned to him and said, 'It's OK, honey, this is a safe place.'

This story, this tragic story, speaks to us of so many things. But as well as the specific details of these particular events, it also speaks to us about two fundamental pillars of our human experience: community and childhood. It speaks of the idea of what childhood is and who brings a child up. Who owns a child? April was Paul and Coral's daughter. But a mass of faceless individuals searched for her as if she was their own. George Monbiot understands why:

'I have never come across a town in Britain that is as child-centred as Machynlleth. The elderly people, in particular, seem to regard the entire population of children almost as if they were their own, doting on them, treating them, offering to babysit and help out. This cataclysm could not have afflicted a more unlikely place, or a place that would feel it more keenly. The entire town seems to have been struck by a family tragedy. There are people on April's estate who look as if they've aged ten years since October. It's as if the lights have gone out from their faces.'

Mid Wales-based author, Jay Griffiths, published her latest book during the summer. It's called *Kith: The Riddle of the Childscape*. In it she looks at childhood and much of that, she says, speaks into the heart of the Machynlleth community. Without referring directly to the town itself, yet alone April's story, one clue she might offer as to why George Monbiot says what he says about the town's child-centeredness, lies in its geography:

'The evidence across cultures and over time is that human nature naturally chooses to nurture childhood in tenderness. It also seems that cultures which are themselves tender to nature are tender to children, themselves a part of nature.'

She gives evidence from various cultures around the world as to 'Who owns a child?' to quote one of her chapter headings. In that chapter, she refers to Welsh heritage.

'Children in traditional Welsh villages used to be considered "village property" and, in Africa, there is one famous saying that "it takes a village to raise a child".'

The Machynlleth experience draws from both the Welsh tradition and the African human experience. It goes a long way to explaining 'why?'. Why the people of this area responded as they did. Why they came out en masse to look for what was, at that point, a little girl who had gone lost. And why, once it was established that she wasn't just lost, the response escalated and intensified to a surprising degree.

On a different child-related issue, others saw this case as highlighting another relevant point. Jackie Bevan from Lancashire, summed this up on her Facebook post.

'I'm probably going to get criticised for this and possibly may be wrong time/wrong place but I have been looking at child abduction figures and according to the England and Wales crime stats 532 children got abducted last year, my question is why is there not as much effort put into finding all these children as there is in April's case? I am in no way saying that they should lessen the effort but isn't every child just as important? If you work the figures out that is just under two children being abducted a day, when do we ever hear of them?'

On another level, leading on from Jackie's point, the academic world sees April's story taking its place in the wider debate about public reaction to child abuse and its coverage in the media. Professor Jenny Kitzinger, from Cardiff University, has consistently argued that the media have a role in the portrayal of cases of child abuse. Having outlined a number of examples of the reporting of such cases, she then sums it up like this:

'Implicit then in all such documentation is an assertion of what childhood really is. Childhood is presented as a time of play, an asexual and peaceful existence within the protective bosom of the family. This image is both ethnocentric and unrealistic. Even while addressing some of the horrors of childhood, these reports confirm myths about the true essence of childhood which contradict the experiences of the majority of young people... Innocence is a powerful and emotive symbol but to use it to provoke public revulsion against sexual abuse is counterproductive. For a start, the notion of childhood innocence is itself a source of titillation for abusers.'

This last point echoes the comments made by others in Machynlleth about the use of pink bows and innocent childlike images of April as part of the public awareness of her plight. No doubt this story will contribute to the furtherance of the debate highlighted by Jenny Kitzinger and others.

Back on the streets of Machynlleth, from such a child-centred spirit as is evident in April's story and in the Machynlleth experience, comes the sense of community seen in so many ways on these pages. The two are hand-in-glove with each other. An awareness of what community means has always been strong in places like Machynlleth. But now, the people in that community see themselves in a different way. It might well be easy to romanticise, but old-fashioned or traditional needn't be equated with sentimental. And certainly not in the context of a child murder. Maybe some are so far removed from such a concept of community they can't comprehend it exists. The voice of one mother from Bryn y Gog is an appropriate way to sum up what the town now feels about itself:

'At the moment, we don't know whether we are fine or not. We have no idea. But the way that we have come together really gets me. It was an amazing thing. You really felt that you were part of a community that would stick together, whatever. If anything was to happen in this town again, we would be able to take this new solidarity and we would come together to face anything. That's a hell of a feeling.'

Kathleen Rogers adds: 'I've been asked countless times, and by reporters quite often, how do we move on? My answer is always, I don't know, but I know that we have to and that we will.'

The community response started with a hope in capitals and in pink. Now it hangs on to a hope of a different kind, no less sincere and genuine, but less spontaneous than that first manifestation. It's a hope built over time, through various stages of development: the Monday, the Sunday, the trial, the verdict, the last month or two. Milestones on the journey to recovery, fuelled by that hope.

Now, even though they are beginning to fragment in the way they are dealing with the grief they have suffered, the people of Machynlleth still have that hope.

Except that now it is a brittle one. Not because of any uncertainty, but because hope now comes from a scared and scarred place and no-one knows exactly how things will work out. It's a fragile hope, that's nearly threadbare for so many. But it will never break.

Pink Ribbons for April is just one of a whole range of publications from Y Lolfa. For a full list of books currently in print, send now for your free copy of our new full-colour catalogue. Or simply surf into our website

www.ylolfa.com

for secure on-line ordering.

yLolfa

TALYBONT CEREDIGION CYMRU SY24 5HE
e-mail ylolfa@ylolfa.com
website www.ylolfa.com
phone (01970) 832 304
fax 832 782